BATTERED

WIVES

Wife-beating is the nation's most common and least-reported crime.

A young woman being beaten by her husband ran screaming for help into the street. The neighbors were annoyed because she was disturbing their peace . . .

Wife-beaters may be the type of men everybody likes —the life of the party!

Only if the number of stitches is sufficiently numerous can an arrest be made . . .

No one pays attention to the battered wife until she reacts desperately and plunges the knife . . .

HAROLD J. PASCAL

THE SECRET SCANDAL:

Battered Wives

ALBA BOOKS

Library of Congress Catalog Card No: 77 - 71027
ISBN 0—8189—1146—8
Copyright, 1977, Alba House Communications,
Canfield, Ohio, 44406

Printed in the United States of America

CONTENTS

Introduction:

The Sickening Statistics   **1**

1. Our Callous Culture   **15**

2. Misleading Myths   **21**

3. Why Does It Happen?   **31**

4. Enter the Police   **49**

5. The Lazy Law   **59**

6. Spreading Cancer   **79**

7. What Can Be Done   **89**

Footnotes   **119**

Useful Addresses   **129**

THE AUTHOR

Following his ordination in 1964, Fr. Harold Pascal spent three years in Latin America as a Vincentian missioner and teacher.

Returning stateside he wrote for some publications, while completing his Ph.D. studies in Counseling Psychology at the University of Miami.

During his stay in Miami, he was a consultant in a nation-wide, federally-funded study on drug-taking behaviour in the U.S. For the past six years he has been actively involved in the National Marriage Encounter movement both in the South Florida and New York areas.

Currently, Fr. Hal is an assistant professor of psychology on the faculty of St. John's University in New York and supervises counselors in the Bronx officer of the Family Consultation Service for the Archdiocese of New York.

DEDICATION

This book was researched and written for all those persons who have sought my professional help in solving the often complex and confusing problems in their lives. Their deep down humanness and appreciativeness have given me a deeper understanding and acceptance of myself and others.

Special thanks are extended to Dr. Barbara Tepa and the Rev. Bud Murray, C.M. for their careful and valuable suggestions in editing the manuscript as well as to Ms. Marion Keyes and Mrs. Dorothy McGowan for their untiring dedication in typing it.

Gratitude also is given to those generous workers who offer such dedicated service to the battered woman and who have provided numerous suggestions and basic research about this problem. To Clare Crawford-Mason and Betsy Steuart in the Washington, D.C. office of the National Broadcasting Company (N.B.C.) who through their concern and labor have offered many valuable leads; to Carolyn Chrisman and Maria Roy of the Abused Women's Aid in Crisis located in New York City; to the thoughtful and resourceful persons of the National Organization of Women; to Sherry Janes, Coordinator of the Women's Transitional Living Center in Fullerton, California; to Joanna Roades, Executive Director of Rainbow Retreat, Inc. of Phoenix, Arizona; to Lynn Olson of the United States Conference of Mayors for her help and to the Ann Arbor-Washtenaw County NOW Wife Assault Task Force for all their helpful labor.

Others who have forwarded their substantive and careful research are my academic colleagues, Murray Straus of the University of New Hampshire, Suzanne Steinmetz of the University of Delaware and Richard Gelles of the University of Rhode Island, to whom I am indebted.

FOREWORD

Let this book be a blessing; let this book be a warning; let this book be an inspiration. Let this book be a guiding light. Let all those who read it, discuss it, pass it on to a neighbor. Let the ideas move from the pages of the book to the minds of the people. Let these thoughts, in turn, pass from beyond the regions of the mind to the arena of the spoken word.

Let every man and woman be touched by the statistics, the case histories, and the elucidation of the myths and causes of wife-beating. Let the police, the attorneys, the judges, the psycho-therapists, the social workers, the physicians, the marriage counselors, the priests, ministers and rabbis who read this book, carry the message with them in their work.

That wife-beating is a heinous, ubiquitous societal problem which can no longer be allowed to go unchecked—that all aspects of the quality of life in our society are affected by the tacit approval of wife-beating—that all members of society commit the sin of omission by neglecting to identify the problem, research the problem, find solutions for it, seek safety for the women and children, and provide help for the men.

That wife-beating is a grave and serious chronic disease which requires emergency treatment, long-term recovery, and preventive measures.

Let this book be a prayer; let this book be a vehicle for peace through understanding; let this book be a peace offering; let this book be a gift to the American public. Let the American public accept this offering of peace with hope in their hearts. Let the children of tomorrow be the children of peace.

Maria Roy

Founder and Executive Director of AWAIC

(Abused Women's Aid in Crisis)

INTRODUCTION:
THE SICKENING STATISTICS

The practice of wife-beating has existed for so long that tradition has dignified it by rhymes and by popular sayings. The traditional argument was clearly written in Blackstone's Commentaries published in 1765 (see chapter on "The Law and Wife-Beating") which allowed a man to beat his wife if he didn't use a stick bigger in diameter than a man's thumb. A plaque in an Indiana motel reads, "a woman, a dog and a walnut tree—the more you beat them, the better they be." Or, consider the popular saying that evidences the acceptability of violence toward wives: "Certain women should be struck frequently, like gongs."

In practically all societies, women have borne an intolerable level of domestic violence. Although there are laws on the books that define an assault and the steps which can be taken to prosecute it, we live out our lives from one generation to the next averting our eyes and minds from the grim facts.[63]

The integral family has always been considered by organized society as a setting where love and gentleness are learned and nurtured. Unquestionably, a healthy home atmosphere still does provide the necessary qualities and training wherein today's infants, children and youths learn the basic virtues that will contribute to a strong, peaceful social structure tomorrow.

But there are some disturbing trends occurring within many families, which probably always have existed but only now appear more frequently in official statistics. One of these trends is wife-beating, which is just beginning to come out of the closet. Wife-beatings coupled with child abuse emphasize the reality that probably no place is more likely to provide violence than the home.

"Domestic muggings" within the family are turning homes into battlegrounds of fights, beatings and even murders as husbands turn on their wives. It is time we began to view the abused wife as a long-suffering innocent person fleeing from a brutal husband, rather than as a complaining nag putting up with an occasional swipe.[98]

Physical cruelty heaped on women need not be tolerated. A husband has not the right by tradition or law to beat his wife. The marriage

2

license is not a "hitting" license. Wife-beating is against the law. Some of the alternatives a woman enjoys instead of being beaten will be mentioned now and will be further elaborated on in this book.

A woman who is battered can call the police, seek the help of a neighbor or family member, or have the locks changed in the home, closing herself in and her husband out. None of these alternatives is air-tight, nor do they necessarily solve the problem. They are stop-gap measures to ward off present threats and attacks. She can hire a lawyer who can ask a judge for an injunction—a court order—to protect herself. If she wishes, a woman may also wear her bruises and breaks and continue to fend off punches and kicks until she has silver threads among the gold. Or she can forgive, try to forget, kiss him and hope she will never be harmed again.[11]

Much investigation has been devoted, rightly, to the sensitive topic of child abuse. Television documentaries, talk shows and numerous magazine and newspaper articles document the sad and tragic plight of battered children. Through these multiple-media, help is sought to solve this frightening problem. But probably one of the major causes for child abuse is wife-beating. The husband who beats his wife often allows his aggressive blows to fall on the bodies of his innocent children. Often a frustrated and battered wife takes out her own frustrations on the children.

A wife remarked in therapy, "You know, I only recently became aware of what was happening in our house. My husband would hit me. I would retaliate by hitting the children, and the children would go outside and kick our dog or chase the neighbor's cat. It's a horrible situation." This vicious circle of family violence is not an uncommon phenomenon. The incidence of family violence is almost as prevalent as the desirable family quality—love.[90] Yet, as a society we shrug our shoulders and consider it an unfortunate problem. Most people misunderstand wife-beating; they either laugh or throw up their hands in despair in trying to work out a viable solution.

Because society tends to sweep wife-abuse under the rug, a beaten woman has fewer avenues of help than a child who is battered by his parents.[106]

Often overlooked but important, is the fact that "violence in the home" links up with "crime in the streets". The person who witnesses or is the victim of family violence finds his own aggressive tendencies increasing. If the individual cannot ventilate these tendencies healthily, he may carry them into the street against an innocent victim. As violence within the walls of the home increases, so does violence in the streets.[95]

The reverse also seems true; the more violence one encounters in society, the more the probability increases that this violence will enter the home. Domestic violence parallels the violence occurring in society generally, a state of affairs which has been referred to as a "murder boom". If the overall murder rate continues to increase in society generally, then murders within families will also go up.

The number of murders in this country jumped from 13,720 in 1968 to 19,510 in 1973. Some 100,020 persons were murdered during this five year period—about twice the number of Americans killed in the Vietnam war.[49] Sometimes violence in a family is turned back on the parents; i.e., Lizzie Borden who in 1892, as this famous rhyme depicts:

> ...took an ax
> And gave her father forty whacks
> When the job was neatly done
> She gave her mother forty-one.[90]

Perhaps, we should ponder our national responsibility. To the degree we as a nation support the use of extreme physical force as a means of social control, we tend to foster physical force as a means to control a wife or a companion.

The nightly T.V. fare for many Americans is violence. If this violence were confined to the realm of fantasy for individuals, it would be acceptable. But, often violence on television only reinforces the notion that the principle pathway to attain justice is through violent behavior. So, if a husband does not think that his wife is being just with him, he can revert to physical abuse to force her to be just.

Until violence within the family is understood and healed, other expressions of violence in American society will continue to flourish.

Wife-beating is the nation's most common and least reported crime.[11] Wife-beating in this book is defined as a woman who has or is receiving deliberate severe and repeated demonstrable physical injury from her husband. The minimal level of injury is evaluated as severe bruising. Without minimizing or underplaying mental cruelty or psychological injury, we are not going to study or evaluate it.

What is known about the number of instances is merely the tip of the iceberg. A Citizen's Dispute Settlement Center in Miami handled nearly a thousand cases of wife-beating during one year. A similar center was opened in affluent Montgomery County, Maryland, where a Citizen's Committee turned up more than 600 cases of wife-beating.[4] In England, Erin Pizzey, a woman who pioneered the establishment of homes for battered wives, estimated that in at least one in every one hundred marriages, severe, repetitive physical assaults on women occur.[46] In Fairfax County, Virginia, of 4,073 family disturbance calls in 1974, 30 a week were from women.[69]

In addition to the actual calls and the complaints filed, unreported incidences would add up to a truer picture of the extent of the problem. Several years ago a study of 40 families was done in Chicago. The 40 families were suspected by police and social service agencies of intra-family violence. As they anticipated, the researchers found numerous cases of wife-beating. They then did a follow-up study on 40 families who were neighbors of the first group. These families had no known history of wife abuse. The researchers were startled to find that more than one-third of these families had histories of wife-battering, five of them on a regular basis.[106]

For every one complaint of assault and battery filed by a wife against her husband, the Sheriff of Washtenaw County, Michigan, maintains there are at least six not filed.[43]

Two researchers attempting to assess the prevalence of physical violence in families studied the cases of applicants for divorce. One found that 17% of his cases spontaneously mentioned overt violent behavior and the other discovered that 23% of the middle-class couples and 40% of the laboring-class couples gave physical abuse as a major complaint.[51,64] This last detail is very important—physical abuse as a major complaint —because although it may not have been listed as a major complaint, such abuse probably occurred more frequently than the usual percentages indicate.

In fact, most authorities consulted on this point believe, that for a true understanding of the incidence of physical abuse in divorce proceedings, percentages cited should be doubled. From personal therapy experience in Family Consultation Agencies both in Miami and New York City, the incidence of physical abuse in troubled and divorcing couples approaches 50%. Many professionals who work in the marriage counseling field estimate that one out of four marriages experiences a recurring pattern of violence and about 60-70% of U.S. marriages have experienced at least one instance of physical violence between spouses.[31, 87, 92]

Amazingly, wife-beating is more common than rape! Most authoritative figures cite wife-beating as occurring three times more often. The latest in-depth analysis of rape claims it is not so much a "sex-trip" as a "power-trip". The rapist is actually engaging in an aggressive, frequently revengeful act directed at women in general or some particular woman from his past, i.e., his mother. Wife-beating and rape may have this in common: both are aggressive, violent behaviors. Incidentally, it is not unlawful for a husband to rape his wife.

Rape is certainly a despicable crime and rightly the perpetrators should receive quick and strict justice. But, it seems that many of the well-intentioned women's rights advocates have concentrated their attention on rape and either ignore or are unaware of the violence visited upon women *within* their homes.[42]

8

Not only is physical abuse within the hallowed walls of the home a tragic reality, but frequently this abuse escalates to include homicidal acts. The largest single category of victims in murder cases is that of family members or relatives.[65] A book on criminal violence asserts that murders take place between family members more than in any other murder-victim relationship.[68] In eighteen societies studying intra-familial homicide, rates were compared with the overall homicide rate. In Denmark, for example, the overall homicide rate is 0.2 per 100,000; whereas the intra-familial homicide rate is about 57%. In the U.S., the overall homicide rate is 7 or 8 per 100,000; as against the intra-familial rate of about 25%.[95]

A U.S. task force in 1965 determined that family killings made up 32% of all homicides, and that one-half of these occurred between spouses. Men were more likely to be killed in the streets, but women were more likely to be murdered in their homes.[48] Last year in the Washington, D.C. area during a three-month period, violence erupted in six different families, taking the lives of 14 persons. In one case practically a whole family was wiped out when a father went on a shooting rampage, killing himself and three of his five children.[49]

One policeman interviewed commented that a wife who is regularly assaulted by her husband stands a fair risk of being murdered by him some day. He noted that about 7 out of 10 murders involve married couples and often the murder is preceded by a number of beatings. Interval House in Toronto revealed one such case where the victim was only 23 years old when she was murdered by her husband. She had met him, when she was 14 years old. He was the son of close friends of her family and she had succumbed to him after he threatened to beat her to a pulp. She claimed that she was so threatened and frightened by him that she could not tell anyone. When she was 16, she became pregnant by him and was forced to reveal his identity. Her parents insisted on an immediate marriage.

The beatings increased early in the marriage, particularly when she disagreed with him about anything. Finally she fled to Interval House where he found her and demanded she return home. She refused. Shortly thereafter, she moved into an apartment of her own, but he found her. One day he arrived, locked the children in a room, then, in a fit of rage, bashed his wife over the head with the stock of a shotgun he had brought with him. He then strangled her with an electric cord, hurled her lifeless body on a bed and fled to the basement of the house where he shot himself.[46]

Not all domestic homicides are committed by husbands. Many women charged with homicide have been systematically beaten and abused until they felt they had reached a point of no return. They pull the trigger or plunge the knife to escape from a demeaning and ugly series of beatings.

Often they receive no help until the deed has

been done. But once the homicide is committed, then public tax dollars flow freely for court and jail costs. But these wives are the exception. In California, in 1971, while 8.7% of male homicide victims were murdered by their wives, 32.8% of female homicide victims were murdered by their husbands.42 In one study of 588 homicide victims, 41% of the women victims were killed by their husbands as compared to only 11% of husbands who were killed by their wives.104 Frequently a woman resorts to this irreversible act after long years of suffering violent attacks against her person; in other words, the deaths were victim precipitated.94

One sickening personal experience came from a family dispute which ended in a homicide. After 32 years of marriage, the wife, provoked through the years with physical beatings, finally retaliated with a kitchen knife. She stabbed her husband to death. When I arrived, the police asked me to speak to her for a few minutes.

The weird peacefulness of the woman after this fatal act seemed to signify the final curtain to a long drawn out drama. All that seemed to matter to her was that it was all over. Another grandmother in her fifties will spend the next five to fifteen years of her life in prison because she got fed up with 30 years of abuse and beat her husband to death with a hammer.

In 1974, there were 13 cases in Washtenaw County in Michigan involving homicides. Six of these cases involved women charged with murdering a husband or a boy-friend. In five of the six cases, years of woman-battering preceded the murders.[43] But, no one paid attention to the wife until she stood with the smoking pistol in her hand. More times than not, the statistics indicate husbands kill their wives. In a single month in Washington, D.C. last year, three women who had reported beatings previously by their husbands were later killed.[4]

The positive and extremely high correlation between wife-beating and homicide seems unmistakable. In a Kansas City Police study, this inextricable relationship was partially validated, since this study examined wife-beating and wife-murder. In 85% of family homicides and aggravated assaults, the police had been called in at least once in the two years prior to the fatal act, and in 50% of the cases, police had been summoned five or more times in the two year period before the murder or aggravated assault occurred.[45]

Supporting the result of this study, as well as the Uniform Crime Reports issued by the Federal Bureau of Investigation (F.B.I.), the New York City Police Department's crime analysis section in their 82-page report showed that in 1975, friends, acquaintances, wives, husbands and other family members committed approximately two-thirds of the murders. Private residences remained the most common place for homicides, accounting for 43.2% of the total.[21, 37]

An important factor in domestic homicides is the prevalence of handguns. One half of all American homes possess one handgun.[6] Domestic violence is not a question of a slap on the face.

Rather, the situation is often one of life or death. Almost as many people were killed during the first six months of 1972 in New York City by a member of their own family as were killed during the previous three years of the "troubles" in Northern Ireland.[93] Even these statistics do not tell the whole story since automobile accidents are a frequent means of spouse murders.

Because domestic violence, particularly wife-battering, is a multi-dimensional problem, many professions, such as law enforcement agencies, attorneys, mental health workers, physicians and social workers have been enlisted in an attempt to understand and lessen the human suffering involved in this syndrome. Many of the viewpoints and much of the expertise recorded in this book are the result of this cooperaticn.

1. OUR CALLOUS CULTURE

How many of us have enjoyed Andy Capp's wife in the cartoons standing at the door in bathrobe and curlers, rolling pin in hand, impatiently waiting to slam her unsuspecting husband over the head when he staggers in at 2:30 A.M. from a night with the boys?

How many of us laughed uproariously at the joke about the husband who was out until 4:00 A.M. with a business associate only to return home to a waiting wife who clobbered him to the extent that he needed hospital attention? When his associate saw him the following day, he asked his injured friend, "What happened?"

The battered associate replied that when he returned home, knowing it was late, he tried to be extra careful not to make a noise. He explained how he turned off the ignition in the car a half block distant from the house and coasted up to the garage door, how he noise-lessly opened and closed the car door, how he took off his shoes before he went up the stairs so as not to disturb his wife, how he undressed in the dark, yet when he lay down next to his wife, she flipped on the light and clobbered him repeatedly with an oak statue he had given her as an anniversary present!

These characterizations are funny, but one of the reasons they are funny is because they are fiction; they almost never happen.

The truth of the matter is the reverse. Frequently, when a husband returns home after a night out with the boys, especially if he was drinking alcohol, the tendency is to wind up the evening by slamming the wife around. Figures released by the Ann Arbor-Washtenaw County Chapter of the National Organization for Women (NOW) following a three-month-long study on wife-beating indicate that for every wife who swings the rolling pin or an oak statue at her mate there are 24 husbands who attack their wives.61

One social worker in Ann Arbor, Michigan, reported that a young woman was being beaten by her husband and ran out in the street screaming for help. The neighbors witnessed the scene, offered no help and, in fact, were annoyed because she disturbed the neighborhood peace!61 One cultural pattern or norm that merits changing is the thinking which maintains that it's all right to beat one's wife. Too many communities view wife-battering as a normal interlude between peaceful and normal husband-wife relationships.

Ingeborg Dedichen, lived with Aristotle Onassis for 12 years. One evening she was severely beaten by Onassis who stopped only because of his own exhaustion. The following day, instead of apologizing, Onassis reflected, "All Greek husbands, I tell you, all Greek men without exception, beat their wives. It's good for them.' And then he laughed.[83]

And then there was the comment made by the bus conductor who had difficulty arranging a seat. He said, "Some of these seats are just like women; you have to kick them to make them work."

The man who beats his wife frequently witnessed his father handling his mother in a similar fashion. It seems normal and in accord with cultural values for these men to beat their wives to keep them in line. After all, his father beat his mother, so it must be all right.

Sometimes the marriage license seems to trigger in men a sense that they possess women as pieces of property. Many wife-beaters begin this unwarranted behavior on the honeymoon just after they receive that piece of paper— the marriage license—which seems to provoke in them a sense of ownership to do with the newly acquired "object" anything they want.

A couple once came for counseling. They had

gone South for their honeymoon many years before and visited for a few days with a sister-in-law. One afternoon the newlywed wife was seated outside the house where they were staying; suddenly her angered husband appeared and, seemingly unprovoked by her in any way, began to beat her viciously with mallet-like fists until she toppled over semiconscious.

Years later, the sister-in-law expressed to this woman her amazement that she remained married to "that man" after such a brutal attack. The battered wife confided that despite having four children during her 21 years of marriage, she never experienced an orgasm after that attack. How many battered women, as a result of a similar violent attack, are turned off sexually from their spouses?

One researcher cites case after case of physical violence being showered upon women and concluded that if these situations were not part of a husband-wife relationship, the man unquestionably would have been arrested for assault.[68]

Our cultural norm of averting our eyes and dangling our arms in the face of physical abuse to wives has caused institutions charged and commissioned to minister to battered wives to fail to protect them effectively. Two University of Michigan law students have documented their research with instances where again and again wife-battering has received implied social approval by police as well as by mental health and social service agencies.[55] These agencies often do nothing even when they have direct knowledge. Physicians and hospitals are required by law to report any known cases of serious injury to the police. But, because spouse assaults are frequently interpreted as being a family problem and a private matter between spouses, these assaults are rarely reported.

Experiments performed on "bystander intervention" conclude that the most important variable is the social definition of correct action for a bystander and not the severity of the crime or concern for the welfare of the victim.[5] Bystanders frequently interpret a man abusing a woman as a family affair and therefore a non-intervention situation. Many persons who did not intervene in the much-publicized Kitty Genovese murder argued that they thought it was a family affair.[77]

Another experiment had couples interact in a standardized and conflicting laboratory task and compared the form of interaction with data for unmarried couples in the same task situation. Result? Strangers were treated more gently and compassionately than were spouses.[79] Other researchers used an experimental task which required a couple to reach a decision, and found that unrelated couples listened respectfully to one another, whereas married couples were often rude to each other.[103]

Although rudeness is not violence, it may escalate to include interspouse violence which begins with rudeness and culminates in physical abuse. Should not this phenomenon of interaction cause us to wonder? Two people who claim to love each other, who want to mutually share their lives and make a firm commitment to real-

19

ize certain goals together, wind up treating one another shabbily, while strangers behave sensitively. This observable behavior is a murky maze, but it needs in-depth exploration if we hope to lessen wife-battering behavior.

2. MISLEADING MYTHS

The major myth about wife-beating is that it is not a problem! Persons or societal institutions seem to deny its existence. But it is gradually surfacing.

Over one hundred years ago, John Stuart Mill wrote a scathing indictment of the possible position of women in marriage in "The Subjection of Women."

"When we consider how vast is the number of men, in any great country, who are little higher than brutes, and that this never prevents them from being able through the law of marriage, to obtain a victim, the breadth and depth of human misery caused in this shape alone by the abuse of the institution swells to something appalling. Yet these are only the extreme cases. They are the lower abysses, but there is a sad succession of depth and depth before reaching them. In domestic as in political tyranny, the case of absolute monsters chiefly illustrates the institution by showing that there is scarcely any horror which may not occur under it if the despot pleases, and thus setting in a strong light what must be the terrible frequency of things only a little less atrocious."[57]

That was a century ago. Only now are true experiences of victims appearing. These personal accounts contain no mythological elements because some of the women have sought shelter in Erin Pizzey's homes for battered women. One woman in her late twenties came to the refuge with her nose broken, most of her teeth missing and her hair falling out. Her husband beat her continually and habitually, put a gun to her head threatening to shoot her. Her youngest son was thrown across the room so often for crying that at the age of three, he was still afraid to speak.

Another slender, red-haired woman with blue eyes claimed her husband disappeared for days without saying why and then punched her when he came back if dinner wasn't ready. She finally left him after he had gone to get an axe, threatening to kill first their dog and then her.[101]

Not only does wife-beating exist. It is one of our major social problems. Some concerned individuals admit its existence, but maintain that an increase in arrests and prosecutions of wifebeaters would result in more poor and minority persons ending up behind bars. *This is a myth. Police in the white middle-class city of Norwalk, Connecticut, receive roughly the same number of wife-abuse calls as police in a Harlem precinct of the same size.*[96]

Wife-beaters come from every race, religion, ethnic background, economic class, educational level and age group. Increased arrests and prosecutions for wife-beaters would not have an adverse impact on any one racial, ethnic or economic group. Well-intentioned civil-libertarians claim that poor and minority groups would be unduly prosecuted. Either they are not aware of the facts or their reaction is a knee-jerk, clenched-fist opposition to arrest, which is not the issue. Rather the issue is equal protection and the non-discriminatory application of the laws.[42]

Mary is blind in her right eye from a vicious kick in the head.... Jane's wrist has been deliberately broken four times.... Elizabeth is practically paralyzed after being slammed against a wall. All of these women lived in middle class homes and neighborhoods.[107]

It is a myth to claim that wife-beating is confined to the lower socio-economic levels of society. Professionals, who work with battered wives maintain that *some of the hard-core and inveterate wife-beaters are attorneys, doctors and business executives.* Abused Women's Aid in Crisis (AWAIC) counselled four women last year whose husbands are Ph.D.'s. Two of them are professors at top universities. A fifth abused woman is married to a very prominent attorney.

Some battered wives enjoy the comfortable surroundings their husbands provide and find it difficult to leave them. Many wives live in expensive suburban homes, send their children to good schools, and vacation in various parts of the world twice a year. Statistically, these women do not come from the lower socio-economic class. It is a misconception to think they do.

A common myth is that any woman who accepts brutal beatings over a period of time evidences serious psychological problems equal to her husband's. Usually this carries with it the idea that the beaten woman is probably masochistic and enjoys her ill-treatment.

There may be isolated cases of women who consider rough handling an indispensable evidence of love, just as there are isolated cases of men who want to be beaten. But the majority of beaten women do not consider a punch in the face a sign of love. The flagellants of the Middle Ages were a small sect who may have derived some sexual satisfaction from physical beatings. Most contemporary women do not receive their sexual fulfillment from a belt buckle.

The testimony of women who attempt to prosecute their husbands for beating them offers no satisfying words, no indications that they enjoyed it or regarded it as an integral part of their lives. For example, some of the reports filed by women contain these claims: Mrs. A. was dragged across the floor by the hair; when she screamed, she was slapped in the face. Mrs. B. was tied to a chair in the basement, her mouth was taped, and her breasts were burned with lighted cigarettes. Mrs. C. was thrown down a flight of stairs, and, as she tried to dial the telephone to summon help, she was punched in the mouth. Mrs. D. was knocked to the ground, kicked, then locked in the trunk of the family car. None of these reports indicate that the women derived any pleasure whatsoever from this abominable treatment, nor did it seem to satisfy any unconscious need.[46]

Some psychiatrists in the past attempted to explain why women need physical abuse. Helene Deutsch argued unconvincingly that all women psycho-biologically possess a passive-masochistic disposition.[16] Sandor Rado reasoned disjointedly that because women are deprived of a penis— a more pleasure-producing organ than theirs— they tend towards masochism.[73]

Perhaps a more insightful portrayal of the true nature of masochism in the feminine psyche is offered by Karen Horney. She contends that cultural factors such as emotional dependence, a conditioned absorption in "love", an inhibition of expansiveness, and a curtailment of autonomous development, exert such a powerful influence on women that it is hard to see how they can escape becoming masochistic to some degree.[40] But to ignore the human suffering involved in wife-beating by claiming that women are masochistic is to deny the facts.

Another often repeated popular myth is that women who are beaten provoke their husbands to beat them. This is coupled with the masochistic approach. Battered women are attacked when they are sleeping, when they return home from shopping, when they are cleaning the house and they search themselves for some clue as to why they were attacked. The fact of the matter is that the husband provokes the attack because of something going on in his head and the wife becomes the victim.

A young woman lived six years with a husband who beat her viciously about twice a year. She said, "I always thought I'd provoked him... that I'd done something to irritate him. I fooled myself... I'd tell myself that he wasn't going to do it again... that I loved him. I'd keep making excuses for him." On one occasion, this young woman, after suffering a vile attack, could not think of anything she could have done to have provoked it. When her husband returned three days later she asked him what, in fact, she had done to irritate him. He answered that he "hadn't seen her in a skirt in months."[61] Professionals may offer various explanations of what was going on in the husband's head but the fact remains that the wife was the victim of an unprovoked attack.

On the other side of this coin (the myth that women provoke attack), is the view that a family member who physically attacks another member is insane or possesses some defect or abnormality.[90] Most evidence indicates that husbands who attack their wives appear *normal* in other aspects of their lives. These men learn to respond to frustration by physically abusing their wives. They are not loners, nor are they friendless. In fact, *they are usually the type of men everybody likes and are the life of the party!* This makes it even harder on the wife, because others would not understand her problems.

Some maintain that in the majority of cases before marriage there are certain indicators which foreshadow a husband's violent behavior. This is a myth. Actually the reverse appears more true; in the majority of cases *there were no indicators* of future abuse. It is true, though, that in some cases the boyfriend begins battering the girlfriend long before marriage. Young girls should be made aware that once a boyfriend begins to beat them the "muggings" don't end once they get married. Often they become more vicious and more frequent.

Another myth is that during their wives' pregnancies men treat them with tenderness and love. Society usually views the conception of a child as a blessed event. Frequently, the general public believes that this event strengthens the love bond between husband and wife. But very often during their wives' pregnancies men commit violent attacks against them. The crisis of pregnancy apparently often leads to acts of physical violence.32

A study by two law students found that 35% of the battered women interviewed reported that they were beaten while they were pregnant and in some cases a mis-carriage was induced.[55] In the Kalamazoo research project, half of the victims were assaulted when they were pregnant.[44] In another study, 80 families were interviewed and in 10 the spouses discussed incidents of violence while the wife was pregnant.[31]

Occasionally a report appears in a local paper affirming the presence in families of this nasty practice, i.e. "A 20-year-old youth accused of strangling his pregnant wife hung himself last night from a knotted bedsheet in his cell at Clinton County Jail..."[32] Reports from Britain indicate that beatings visited on pregnant wives by their spouses are relatively common.[63]

Interviews with women provide insights as to why their husbands batter them during pregnancy. Some men are sexually frustrated because they superstitiously refrain from sexual relations during a wife's pregnancy. Other men experience an increase in stress and tension when they realize the economic strain that will result from a new family member and think they can release this by beating-up their wives. Many of these women became pregnant before marriage, which created stress for the husband because the couple's new-found routine would be radically interrupted by a newcomer. Some women explained that the beatings were due to their own irritability and critical attitude towards their husbands because of the bio-chemical changes of pregnancy. Some men also engage in prenatal child-abuse which they frequently hope will terminate the pregnancy with a miscarriage instead of asking their wives to undergo the usually morally unacceptable alternative—abortion. These men simply do not want a child or another child. A pregnant woman is also more vulnerable to attack, and therefore a husband may batter his pregnant wife, knowing that she is unwilling or unable to retaliate.[32]

3. WHY DOES IT HAPPEN ?

Why do some men physically abuse their wives? Why do their wives tolerate being beaten? Probably there are as many answers to these questions as there are persons involved. Researchers and practitioners propose a number of reasons which shine light on the muddied waters of personal motivation.

In many cases, the frequently hidden destructive forces of marriage which secretly undermine it are seen through the sprouting of disappointments, distrust, hostility, hatred and physical abuse. How many persons enter marriage thinking or saying they will develop unpleasant traits in themselves or in their partners? Very few, probably none. How, then, do undesirable traits which choke a marital relationship develop?

Human limitations are one reason; another is

an individual's personal neurosis. A third reason is the security of the position in marriage, which can be compared to a civil servant's job; as long as the party perseveres, he is assured of the position. A fourth is the inadequate preparation or education prior to marriage: most preparation consists only of the subtle conditioning processes that accompany a person's experiences of growing up in a family.

A fifth reason resides in contradictory expectations, whether within an individual or between the marital partners. A disrupted relationship resulting in violence can also develop because of faulty sexual ideas particularly about the opposite sex.[40] Some of these reasons are general. Now we will discuss some more particular reasons.

Some men experience their own limitations acutely and believe that alcohol will in some way overcome their inadequacies. The evidence of the presence of alcohol in wife-beating situations is contradictory. Some researchers claim that alcohol drinking husbands account for 90% of the wife-batterers; others maintain that few wife-beaters drink alcohol and are usually cold sober when they beat their wives.[4, 6, 27, 44, 46, 49, 61, 98]

Rainbow Retreat in Phoenix, Arizona intimately associates a husband's alcohol abuse with family violence.[74] Trudy Don of Interval House located in Toronto, Canada, maintains that once a man becomes a wife-beater no one knows where his violence will end, especially if he is a heavy drinker—nine out of ten wife-beaters have a booze problem. After several drinks, they lose all restraint, their fury is unleashed and they go berserk.[46]

One woman who was viciously beaten several times claimed that her husband was the perfect man—except when drunk! She was legally advised to leave him; but she could not. In some mysterious way, he was necessary for her well-being.[98]

Another study indicated that the wives interviewed complained that their husbands drank alcohol frequently, gambled regularly and that unemployment was a regular feature of their life-styles.[11] Another professional noted that a wife-beater is often an intemperate drinker who experiences guilt about actions committed while drunk.

A further study offered a composite mosaic of the case histories of wife-beaters by describing them as men with low frustration tolerance who often completely lose control under the influence of alcohol. They punch and kick their wives in a savage manner, perhaps using weapons to aid their assault.

At times, these men rush into marriage with idealistic notions of creating a truly happy family atmosphere. Children are welcomed and nurtured at first, but when coping becomes difficult and frustrations are experienced, they resort to violence.[46] Some beaten wives were interviewed in another study to ascertain their husbands' characteristics. The women responded that a number of attacks occurred when their husbands were drunk.27

The other side of the issue, that wife-beatings occur most often when the husband is sober, was presented by a task force to the Montgomery County Council in Maryland last year. This task force reported that only a small proportion of the women commented that their husbands were drinking at the time of the violence which, as the task force pointed out, "contradicts a widely accepted stereotype of wife-beaters."6 A number of marriage counselors interviewed in preparation for this book believed that some wife-beaters are chronically excessive drinkers, but that others (which they indicated are in the majority), drink to lower the level of their inhibitions and so do what they wanted to do all along, namely, to physically abuse their wives.

If a man abuses alcohol the chances that he will abuse his wife increase tremendously. Professionals who work with marital problems would do well to explore these associated areas in order to render effective help to persons caught in this abusive web.

Some wife-beaters are neurotic. They store up a pathological anger within themselves which they eventually take out on a female—their wife. This type of person usually hates himself and displaces his rage at himself onto his wife.105, 106

A study of four assaulters, black males ranging in age from 34 to 47 years old who were members of the lower socio-economic class, generally revealed a past characterized by a domineering, rejecting mother relationship. These persons' reactions during their youth were usually a passive submission to maternal authority coupled with intense efforts to prevent their anger from reaching conscious levels.[81] Rollo May asserts that violence does not arise out of power-lessness...it is the expression of impotence.[54]

Typically jealous slayers are husbands who, after more than five years of marriage, begin to suspect that their wives no longer love them. They convince themselves, with or without evidence, that their wives are unfaithful. One woman, a 29-year-old mother of two children, showed up late one night at the hospital with her eyes blackened and her nose smashed relating this blood-chilling story:

Since her second child had arrived, three years before, her husband had begun to drink heavily and had become more abusive. He ordered her not to eat at the table with him and the children. If she disobeyed these orders, he would hurl her to the floor or slap her around. When she fondled or kissed the children, he would push her away, punch her and scream, "Don't touch these kids, you filthy whore. You'll give them a terrible disease."[46]

Some wife-beaters deteriorate mentally beyond a neurosis. These men are mentally ill, such as the paranoid husband who interpreted every

phone call his wife made, every letter she received, as a conspiracy to commit adultery. He frequently beat her in fits of jealousy. The woman's
ordeal ended when he was committed to a mental
hospital as a paranoid schizophrenic. But this is
not the average wife-beater; he is not usually
psychotic.

There exists a cultural norm that expects men
to act masculine by using physical strength. One
aspect of machismo in Latin societies is the ability
to dominate the female. If this physical strength
bit is carried too far, it can result in a neurotic
concern for physical superiority over a female.
Some individuals who are labeled as violent or
tough may attempt to live up to their self-image
by practicing violence. Due to past beatings, the
wife may also flinch when an argument begins,
which provides a cue for the husband to beat
her.[89, 91, 94]

A certain amount of violence has been essential
to the masculine image. In the movie *Play It
Again, Sam*, Woody Allen caricatures this attitude when the Humphrey Bogart character says
he never met a woman who didn't understand "a
slap in the mouth and a slug from a .45."[18]

An appropriate amount of physical aggression
is part and parcel of living in this world, but a
compulsive masculinity can develop in males.
Cross-cultural and intracultural society studies
show that this neurosis develops often when a
father is physically or psychologically absent.[93, 95]
The low salience of a father figure or his absence

has been found to be associated with the male child's desire to subordinate women and the glorification of physical aggression.

A subtle nuance is added to this masculine image factor when one considers the husband who lacks a certain amount of aggression or who cannot maintain his leadership role in the family. Studies indicate that when the male cannot be leader in the family, marital dissatisfaction results. Not only are the members of the family unhappy, but this type of husband also often resorts to physical force to attain his supposed dominant position.[86, 91]

The familial interaction can produce violence, rather than the violence being a chance occurrence or the product of a psychotic personality. One can see that a healthy male image contains a certain degree of aggression. Yet the individual need not engage in a compulsive masculine approach to the female to bolster his own lack of leadership. The healthy male expresses his masculinity with respect for his female partner.

In some instances, men harbor hostility towards women. Three psychologists from Michigan State University staged a series of fights that were to be witnessed by unsuspecting passersby. This experiment was done to assess the reaction of men who watch a violent act against a woman. The researchers found to their amazement that male witnesses rushed to the aid of men being assaulted by either men or women and that men helped women being hit by other women. But not one male bystander interfered when a male actor apparently beat up a woman.[71] Various interpretations can be offered for this type of behavior: perhaps, the cultural norm of non-interference in apparent marital disputes holds true or these subjects believed that women need physical punishment from time to time. Perhaps a hostile attitude towards women exists in various males.

A discordant or troubled relationship between a husband and wife sometimes relates back to their relationship with significant others during their formative years. Even though some men value and esteem women as human persons, they may harbor deep within themselves a secret distrust of them; this distrust frequently emerges in their psyches as a result of a faulty relationship with their mothers during their formative years.

Emotionally, men who batter their wives are usually excessively possessive and do not allow them to enjoy any friends. This abnormal possessiveness often blossoms into a quasi-insane jealousy which results in reigning down blows on an innocent victim for supposed infidelities. This male behavior also evidences a deep insecurity which probably relates back to a disrupted or fragmented relationship with the most significant female in the wife batterer's early life— his mother.

Faulty sexual ideas, particularly about the opposite sex can also cause men to react violently. Only a single study will be cited here illustrating one aspect of a male's faulty sexual ideas.

A physician was playing with a ball, which as she showed the children, had a slit in it. She pulled the edges of the slit apart and put her finger in, so that it was held fast. Of the 28 boys she asked to do the same, only six did it without fear and eight could not be induced to do it at all. Of the 19 girls, nine put their fingers in without a trace of fear; the rest showed a slight uneasiness, but none of them displayed serious anxiety.[40]

A man who has been unable or never had the opportunity to work through an anxiety such as vagina dread can eventually be provoked by this dread and displace his anxiety onto his wife by beating her. Granted, this syndrome is exemplified solely by this one example. Only some boys in the experiment reacted negatively and perhaps as they mature, they will correct this attitude. But, if one reflects on the many aspects of sexual contact and the many unhealthy attitudes that already have emerged in various men's psyches, it is understandable how these faulty sexual ideas can lead some men to allay their anxieties by beating up their wives.

If the masculine mystique that hardens men into their turtle-like shells of incommunicable suffering can be cracked, then the why of wife-beating behaviors can be solved. Many men find it difficult to communicate their distress to their wives or to a professional counselor because they believe it is unmanly to do so. They think that if they can't solve their own problems without outside help then they are unmasculine. This attitude, reinforced by cultural norms, prolongs their inner anguish and their overt self-defeating behavior of beating their wives.

If these men would communicate their frustrations without the need to use alcohol as an escape, then their abusive behavior could be controlled. If they could communicate their neurotic needs, understand them and take practical steps to change, then these abnormal needs could be checked and sublimated. Faulty sexual ideas could be corrected and with a cooperative wife, their mutual sexual experiences could become satisfying. But these goals need to be shared mutually by husband and wife through communication and an honest effort to change.

We will now investigate the why of women who receive beatings. Why do women remain in a situation where they frequently receive physical abuse? Again, there are probably as many answers to that question as there are beaten women.

Economically, women are dependent on their husbands. Frequently, battered women have not been working and think they have no saleable skill with which to support their families if they decide to leave. They often have low self esteem and feel incapable in the work-a-day world. As children, many women are raised to feel they are incomplete persons. They are often treated as second-class members of a family in interest, achievement, education and resources in comparison to their brothers. Frequently, they are indoctrinated to think that their goal in life is to please the man, to support the male in his quest for success.

Some women, because of this learned and scripted childhood inferiority, seek out punishment as their natural due. Their perceived lack of the necessary talents to earn a living as a working person leaves them deflated and depressed. Divorce for these women means poverty. Those who belong to the lower class seem to be able to survive economically more readily than the middle and upper class, because the former usually receive welfare payments, whereas the latter do not want this type of support. If these women do divorce, default on support payments is such a common phenomenon that they don't know how to hold the family together.

Other women stay in horrific marriages for the sake of the children. They believe that at least the husband puts a roof over the head of the children and food on the table. Some also think that it is better to have a violent husband who is around the house however infrequently than no father-image at all.

A woman who is now in the process of obtaining a divorce spent 15 years living with an abusive alcoholic. She said that she stayed for the sake of the children. She visualized herself as unable to raise the children without him since she had no work record to fall back on. She married him immediately after graduation from high school and found it very difficult to think about venturing out on her own.

Her husband would also threaten to do things to her if she left him and she had no reason to doubt him. Furthermore, she felt it would be immature to walk out on her marriage. She said she was trained "to cater to a man." As her two boys grew older, they began to sleep with knives hanging from the sides of their beds. The older one eventually kept a loaded ".22" under his bed. Both of these boys now have difficulty with school. Reflecting on her married years, she said, "You'd be surprised what women will do to keep the peace until the children grow up."61

A societal value which may lead women to remain in an ever worsening situation insists that children cannot be brought up by one parent, particularly the woman. The idea is frequently expressed that a single parent household robs the children of a healthy family interaction. If the interaction between the family members is healthy, then this belief may have some validity. But when a woman is beaten by her husband, *this can only result in children experiencing emotional and psychological pain that leaves indelible, negative scars.*

Another societal value or norm which programs women to "hang in" is the oft-repeated notion that the wifely role is the pre-eminent role for women, the most important and ideally the most fulfilling. American thinking supports the belief that a woman cannot be a "total woman" unless she is married. Many women believe that if they fail at marriage, they fail as women. A woman is divorced less readily than a man since the social stigma of being a divorcee carries certain immoral overtones. These implications frequently constrain a woman to remain in a violent marriage.

Some Catholic women, because of their religious up-bringing, also see no way out of a violent marriage. They believe that their marriage vows, "for better or for worse," were made for life and that they must accept this worsening situation. For these women, it is an energy-consuming struggle between their religious ideal and the real violence they experience which tells them there is no marriage where love has died. Moreover, this daily battle within themselves frequently gives them the appearance of the neurotic housewife.

A number of other women have been conditioned to accept physical abuse from their husbands because they saw their mothers receive the same treatment. These women feel they can do nothing about the violence visited upon them except to do what their mothers did: "to put up with it."

Some of the feelings encountered in such women explain their inner sufferings. Fear is probably their main emotion. They fear being on their own, the responsibility for the children, the need to work and vengeance on the part of the husband. Many of them experience anger which they direct at their assailants. Others may internalize their anger and become depressed, a depression which may deepen to the degree that the women contemplate suicide.

They may even begin to doubt their own sanity and to isolate themselves from all normal human contact resulting in their belief that they are losing control. Sometimes guilt overcomes these women because they blame themselves for the beatings they receive. Another common feeling is embarrassment. They are embarrassed to think, and to admit, that they chose a physically abusive man. When they need to consult their family doctors due to the injuries sustained, many claim that they have been in a car accident or that they fell when they had too much to drink.

Battered women are troubled in various ways. Sixty-per cent of one sample of women interviewed said they were pregnant at the time of their marriage.[27] One expert in wife-battering noted that some women who are involved in violent marriages are "extremely provocative, promiscuous, and inadequate to the task of managing a household." Sometimes, these self-defeating behaviors occur as a result of unpleasant experiences with the opposite sex during the formative years of life.

During infancy, a young girl may experience the many frustrations of being rebuffed, betrayed, told lies, relegated to second place in favor of a male sibling or parent, threatened and intimidated. She reacts by creating fantasies of aggression: stealing, choking, burning, cutting and killing.[40] These childhood conflicts can spill over into her relationship to men in later life.

A little girl may be badly hurt through some great disappointment from her father. This may transform her desire to receive from her man into a vindictive urge to take from him by force. The latter attitude, formed by her earlier experiences, will transform her life into a drive to harm the male or exploit him. A documented case explained the feelings of displacement a young girl carried into adulthood when a younger brother was born. Her envy, however, focused on his penis which generalized to an attitude of revenge against men in general. Once the displacement was canceled, she was able to be a true woman and her revenge dissipated itself.[40] May not this conscious or unconscious dynamic be present in some women who suffer beatings from their husbands?

Suppose the wife responds with a reaction formation of excessive modesty which masks the repressed desire for power. This will eventually result in a depression because her real wishes remain unfulfilled. She becomes childlike and helpless, an attitude through which she eventually dominates her man. As a consequence, the husband is often thrown into a deeper depression than his partner because she throws the entire responsibility for her helplessness onto him, robbing him of the breath of life.

Some women's impaired relationships with men are revealed in indifference or morbid jealousy, in distrust or irritability, in claims or feelings of inferiority, in a need for lovers or for intimate friendships with women, all of which have one thing in common—the incapacity for a full—both body and soul—love relationship with a heterosexual love object. As a result, a type of guerrilla warfare frequently exists in a marital relationship wherein the woman constantly wages an envious and revengeful battle.[40]

But the majority of women "mugged" by their husbands in their own homes seem to be gentle persons who unluckily marry violent men. A certain proportion of these women are well-educated—nurses, teachers, professionals—and they often seem to display a "savior" mentality. They knew frequently before the marriage that their men were violent, but they thought that afterwards they would be able to redeem and change them. This "savior" mentality is similar to those women who marry drunks to reform them, but who unfortunately end up in the vortex of the problem, receiving most of the abuse.

Battered women remain in a physically abusive marriage for a variety of reasons, including their own fears of trying to "make it" on their own as well as for the sake of the children. *But one of the principle reasons remains the cultural norm that tolerates a man who beats his wife.* Unless persons in society become more conscious of the wrongness of wife-beating and attempt to offer viable alternatives to women caught in this upward cycle of abuse, we will only have increased violence in the home and, as a result, on the streets.

4. ENTER THE POLICE

Although the first person on the scene in a "domestic mugging" situation is usually the police officer, his role is frequently that of after-the-fact intervention. In fact, one study done in New Haven, Connecticut, found that in 38% of family disputes one party had departed before the police arrived.96 If the officer witnesses a misdemeanor or a felony in progress, he may arrest. If he does not witness either crime, the victim may still file a complaint.

Traditionally, the police separate the combatants, attempt to restore order, inform the wife that she can file a complaint and then return to other duties. Officers sometimes interview the victim immediately; others have a policy of interviewing the wife the following day, and still others will not interview until a "five day cooling off period" ends. This "cooling off" procedure is used in Washington, D.C. In approximately 7,500 incidents against women in 1966, less than 200 of them felt they had secured their objective.[24]

Whatever the practice may be in the local community where the battered wife lives, she should always see to it that the report is taken even if five days have elapsed. She would be well advised, when calling the police, to say that she is about to be or has already been abused by a "man." She should not use the word "husband" because some police departments ignore domestic violence calls and others relegate them to Class "C" status (which means that when there is time they will get around to them). She should simply say, "there's a violent man in the home who is threatening me or beating me."

A process, known as "screening," is used by a number of police departments, and usually proceeds in this way: if a woman calls the police seeking protection from her husband's assault, the precinct operator asks if the husband has a weapon. If the woman says "no," the operator will respond that there is nothing the police can do. If she responds that "yes" the husband has a weapon, but on their arrival police find no obvious weapon, they will leave the scene even though the assault is still going on!

If the woman insists that her husband be arrested, the case is referred to the prosecutor whose offices are open between Monday and Friday. If she prefers charges on Friday night— and many beatings do occur on week-end nights

—she still has to live with her husband, even during the violent assaults, until Monday morning.[48] *No wonder so few women prefer charges, when the protection of the law is so labored and so often delayed!*

Charles Campbell, a Toronto lawyer who has just completed a book on family law, comments that the police often take a casual view of domestic violence. In some instances they even respond contemptuously towards the battered wife. Though women are often badly beaten as a result of marital fights some policemen are loath to interfere and reluctant to take the initiative in establishing a charge. They may also fail to inform the woman of her right to demand a citizen's arrest. On the other hand, the wife who presses a charge can be in peril, since a month or two may intervene before she and her husband appear in court. During this interval, she usually is living with the man who may threaten and harass her.[46]

A woman seen in therapy experienced this predicament. Her husband, an ex-convict, battered her throughout their marriage. When she finally brought charges, he again threatened to beat her badly or even to kill her. When the police arrived on the scene, he reverted chameleon-like to a meek and pliant manner. He explained that his wife was a mentally ill person and frequently suffered attacks in which she accused him of violent behavior. After the police left, the husband gave his wife the silent, sullen treatment, frequently prowled around the house at night and began to take valuable objects from the house, which she missed but could say nothing about for fear of retaliation.

Robert Shuman, a Sacramento, California Legal Aid Society attorney, claims there is ample evidence that the police sometimes fail to show up when called to intervene in a domestic dispute. They deny the charge.[80] Some police departments have even established ground rules evaluating the severity of the abuse according to the number of stitches a wife receives. *Only if the number of stitches is sufficiently numerous can an arrest be made!*[24]

A woman phoned the San Jose Police Department to report that her estranged husband had just called to say he was coming to her apartment to kill her. She had called at least 20 times during the previous year with similar complaints and on one prior occasion, they had arrested her husband. This time, however, they refused to send aid. Her husband arrived 45 minutes later and stabbed her to death.[39]

Often the reason cited for police non-intervention in a domestic dispute is the high incidence of injuries sustained in answering these calls. Unquestionably, the police have a risky job intervening in family disputes, since often it is possible that the two, husband and wife, will turn on the policeman!

Members of the Toronto Metro police, attempting to rescue a battered wife, have been bitten by the wife and pinned to the floor by the husband while the wife repeatedly kicked them.[46] F.B.I. crime statistics reveal that between 1961 and

1970 in the U.S. 98 officers were killed responding to family violence calls, which was nearly one-sixth of all officers' deaths during that period.21 This high fatality rate can be partially explained by the fact that domestic violence constitutes approximately one-sixth of all police intervention in general.45

A legal researcher estimates that more police calls involve family conflict than do calls for all criminal incidents, including murders, rapes, non-family assaults, robberies, and muggings.68 Another reason may be that police are not sufficiently trained in techniques of effective family intervention. And a frequently cited reason for police non-intervention is "tradition". This traditional argument was clearly written in Blackstone's *Commentaries,* published in 1765:

The husband also, by the old law, might give his wife moderate correction. For, as he is to answer for her mis-behavior, the law thought it reasonable to entrust him with this power of restraining her by domestic chastizement ... The civil law gave the husband the same, or a larger author-ity over his wife; allowing him, for some misdemeanors, with whips and clubs sharply to beat his wife , ... and for others moderate correction.57

The law has changed since Blackstone's day and husbands have no right under criminal law to physically chastize their wives for real or sup-posed misdeeds, but the tradition continues in effect. It preserves, in one form or another, the old common law doctrine of spousal immunity, based on the attitude that since a married couple is legally one entity, one spouse is incompetent to testify against the other.

Today, some states allow one spouse to testify against another in a civil proceeding as well as in a criminal proceeding, but, although spousal immunity has been formally relaxed in the incidents of family violence, in behavioral terms the situation has not changed radically from Blackstone's day. Wives still receive much of the blame for being beaten.[42] A sizable number of policemen still believes that the law stipulates that a husband can strike his wife.[12, 99]

Another factor frequently mentioned is that complaining wives often decide, even as late as the end of the trial, not to testify against their offending husbands. One situation exemplifying how wives tend to drop charges was that of the lady whose face was beaten to a bloody pulp and whose husband had almost succeeded in strangling her when the police broke into her apartment. Three weeks later in court she claimed that her injuries were caused by a fall down a flight of stairs. She testified that her husband didn't lay a hand on her.[46] Such vacillation is not uncommon and many policemen cite it as a reason for non-intervention.

Many police departments use as a guide in wife-beating intervention the International Association of Police Chiefs' Training Bulletin which states, "Avoid arrest if possible. Appeal to the woman's vanity. Explain the procedure of issuing a warrant...and the cost of the court. Explain that (women's) a t t i t u d e s (about pressing charges) usually change by court time. Attempt to smooth feelings, pacify the parties. Remember the officer should never create a police problem where there is only a family problem existing."[48]

As can be noted, most of the advice in this bulletin attempts *to discourage the wife from taking any action*. The cultural norm of considering wife battering a family matter is strongly reinforced; wife-beating should be considered neither an assault nor a court problem.

Here is an actual complaint filed in Ann Arbor, Michigan:

Victim stated the first argument started over a pack of cigarettes. Victim stated accused (her husband) held her against the bathroom wall by the hair and continued to beat victim with his right hand. Victim was six months pregnant at this time. Victim stated accused kept telling victim, "Bitch, you are going to lose that baby," and then the accused would beat victim in the stomach again. After the assault in the bathroom accused told victim to cook dinner. Victim stated accused picked up a butcher knife and put it to the victim's throat and told victim, "I am going to kill you and you know I can do it too, don't you?" Victim answered, "Yes", and accused laid the butcher knife down on the table and turned around and hit the victim in the face with his fist and knocked victim to the floor. Then the accused sat down on victim's stomach and put his knees on victim's arms so victim could not block any licks from accused. The accused started beating victim in the head, face, and stomach. The accused got to his feet and told victim to get up. Victim stated she tried, but was unable to do so and fell back to the floor. The accused started beating and kicking the victim and kicked a kitchen chair over on victims stomach. Victim stated she blacked out. Victim states when she regained consciousness the accused was still beating her.[1]

Can the police not intervene in situations such as this? No matter what reason (s) may be offered for non-intervention, they cannot justify a hands off policy when a wife is assaulted. In the case cited, the woman, after regaining consciousness, did call the police and did sign a complaint. *Unfortunately, the majority of such cases either go unreported or the police apply the suggestions spelled out in the Police Chiefs' Training Bulletin cited above, which for all practical purposes mean inaction.*

The San Francisco Police Department's Director of the Family Intervention Program claims that only one police officer sustained an injury since the training program was instituted. Clearly, this is a benefit to the police officer as well as for the violent husband who avoids arrest. *But is it a benefit for the battered wife?* A reduction in the number of wife-beating men arrested, without corresponding figures to show a reduction in the number of attacks, can hardly be considered a benefit for the victims. In fact, the California Council on Criminal Justice in its evaluation of the program indicated that the police training did not reduce the number of persons who became involved with the criminal justice system as a result of family fights.

Another factor not specified in police reports is how many police injuries were sustained during an arrest following a domestic mugging. It is reasonable to assume that if less men are being arrested for wife-beating, then perhaps less injuries are sustained by the police. It is necessary to make these assumptions because separate statistics are not available.

In San Francisco, California, as in many other cities nationwide, there is no way to distinguish the number of cases involving wives as victims of their husbands under the headings "Aggravated Assault" and "Other Assault." *There are no separate statistics available* on the number of family violence calls received by the police, the number of calls answered, the average time lapse in responding to family calls, the number of cases for which no report is filed, the number of repeat calls, the number of arrests arising from a family violence call, and the number of aggravated assaults and homicides resulting from repeat call situations.

According to statistics compiled by Lieutenant Ellis of the San Francisco Homicide Bureau in 1974, over one-fourth of the murders in San Francisco involved enforcing the laws in regard to family violence perpetrated against women; when this occurs, then the discriminatory effect of not keeping statistics is evident.[42]

It is not the purpose of these criticisms to undermine or question the validity of training police officers in effective psychological techniques to reduce the trauma encountered in wife-beating cases. Professional training for police officers should be continually updated to include advanced procedures in handling wife-beating cases judiciously. What is being questioned is the pattern found in so many police departments of unscientific procedures, wherein no clear picture emerges of the effectiveness of training programs to reduce wife-beating practices.

57

In interviews conducted by the staff members and volunteers at the Women's Litigation Unit and the Domestic Relations Unit of the San Francisco Neighborhood Legal Assistance Foundation, victimized women unanimously agreed that they would like the police to respond, whenever called, and to arrive as quickly as possible to prevent serious injuries.

Most of the interviewed thought arrest would be desirable, especially when the beating was in violation of a restraining order or when the victim requested an arrest or when she requested to make a citizen's arrest. As offenders about to be arrested are given the Miranda warning by police, so should women be informed by the police of their right to make a citizen's arrest.[42]

A serious re-evaluation of present police intervention policies in family disputes needs to be inaugurated speedily. The uneven and frequently ineffective procedures employed by many local police in handling family fights and domestic muggings not only paves the way for an escalation of family violence, but also produces unnecessary injury and frustration for many police officers. The present programs that train police officers to intervene in family disputes need careful scrutiny to ascertain whether they actually do reduce family violence.

5. THE LAZY LAW

The federal government protects women in employment and education, but one of the areas which lacks a federal mandate for equal treatment regardless of sex is criminal law. Though individual cases have been won in litigation, the progress toward equality of treatment in criminal law cases has been inconsistent and slow.

At the present time, the law is ineffective in helping a battered woman because it is still based on the idea of a woman as a man's chattel or piece of property, which he can use as he sees fit. *Incredibly, women who are beaten, knifed, sexually mutilated, or otherwise attacked by their husbands have virtually no effective legal protection or recourse!*[42]

Besides the idea of a woman being a piece of property, wife-beating is frequently perceived as a domestic disturbance that the wife somehow tolerates, provokes, or likes in some masochistic way.[48] The law sometimes seems to legitimize a husband's assault. A case was heard in Flint, Michigan, involving a man charged with assaulting his wife. A policeman who was on the scene testified with the wife against her husband. The judge threw out the case claiming that a man's house is his castle and that the police were trespassing![43]

Some women do not seek the protection of the law because of misconceptions about the criminal justice system. One misconception is that a husband has a legal right to beat them. These women actually believe that the marriage contract bestows upon the husband the right to be abusive! Another mistaken idea is that if they leave the house, even after a severe beating, they can be charged with desertion. These views paralyze action by women who, as a consequence, become completely dominated by their violent husbands.

A survey of assault cases in the District of Columbia criminal justice system showed that three-fourths of the cases not involving husbands and wives went to disposition on the merits of the guilt or innocence of the parties involved. But, in husband-wife cases the pattern was completely reversed. Only about one-sixth of all arrests involving marital violence finally ended in trial or with a guilty plea, and the crime charged was invariably a misdemeanor rather than a felony.[24]

The principal problem, prevalent nationwide, is that women whose husbands beat them—frequently on a regular schedule—have no *effective* remedy within the criminal justice system as it now operates. *The problem is not that there are no laws, but that the laws remain unenforced.* There are laws that deal with assault, battery, felony assault, felony wife-beating, disturbing the peace, trespassing, injuring persons or property, and threatening to commit a crime. *"Domestic mugging" is ignored, blamed on the wife or seen as a family affair* and very often allowed to occur.[42]

It will be worth while taking a closer look at the criminal justice system to examine the various alternatives and procedures a battered wife may pursue in her search for justice and peace. This will not be an easy journey: the road contains many man-made obstacles which impede women's attempts to stop their husbands' physical assaults.

After police intervention or nonintervention, as already examined, the victim (if her story is taken seriously), may sign a warrant or complaint. The warrant is then presented by the police officer to an assistant prosecuting attorney. Usually this gentleman begins the same course of action as the police did: trying to pacify the woman. If this is nonproductive, he will frequently insist that she show her sincerity about pressing charges by immediately beginning divorce proceedings.[76]

A case occurred in a Detroit circuit court, where a woman charged her husband with criminal assault, but later withdrew her charge with the explanation that the beating was not bad enough. It was the prosecutor who had informed her that *her case was not strong enough!* What had the husband done that was not strong enough for legal action? *He had tied his wife to the bed and slashed her genitals with a knife.*[43]

Another prosecutor explained that he could offer no protection to the woman. He asked her if the husband would be angry if the warrant were served, if there were a trial, and if he went to prison. Then, he further questioned whether her husband would be angry after he was released from prison. With this type of loaded questioning, it is hard to imagine a woman proceeding with the warrant and the arrest. Of course, the answers to the above questions are frequently affirmative and the prosecutor counsels the wife to try to patch up the marriage for her and the children's safety.[48]

Although numerous prosecutors conduct preliminary interviews of wife-beating episodes in this fashion, once the wife adamantly begins the process it is absolutely necessary to follow through with all the court proceedings, no matter what the hassle or the time involved. Not following through on the wife's part is *an invitation to more abuse and battering.* If the wife does pursue the issue, then the husband and society receive the message *that it's not acceptable to beat another person, even if that other person is one's wife.*

If the wife continues her quest for justice and the assistant prosecutor decides after their interview that criminal charges can be brought, then a warrant will be recommended and signed by the assistant prosecutor. For a warrant to be recommended, the facts must show that a crime was committed under the laws of the state, that the accused committed the crime, and that it is in the best interest of justice and the public to take the case to court.

The prosecutor decides exactly which criminal law has been broken. After he signs the warrant, the police officer takes it to the district court judge in the district where the crime occurred. If the judge decides to sign the warrant, the police look for the subject and an arrest may follow.[76] This entire process of seeking a warrant is time-consuming and often nerve-racking. The wife frequently decides that the warrant for her spouse's arrest will probably cause more trouble than it is worth and drops the action.

Another route to remove the assailant from the vicinity of the victim is a citizen's arrest. Since the majority of family disputes involve misdemeanor offenses such as assault and battery, which need to be witnessed before an arrest can be made, the citizen's arrest seems the only quick and effective method to realize this goal. The steps required in making a citizen's arrest are: first, a plain request to make a citizen's arrest; second, a description of the crime witnessed by the citizen; and third, some "pointing out" of the accused to the police. To ensure that an accuser will not be brought up on charges for a false citizen's arrest, she must prove that she acted in good faith. It seems entirely justifiable and necessary that police as well as private citizens use citizen's arrest more frequently, especially in wife-beating situations, which so often result in wife-killing tragedies.[42]

It is worth mentioning that once a wife initiates legal action or desires intervention by legal authorities, then she must be prepared to insist that a complaint be signed and an arrest be made. She must realize that these are only the first steps in a long journey which may extend for years. It is well to remember, also, that a complaint may go unheeded, since prosecutors are not compelled to issue a warrant and charge a person with a crime. In some cases, the wife may have to insist that the prosecuting attorney or the district attorney issue the warrant.[76]

Many district attorneys claim that they do not issue warrants because their cases are often very weak. Their inherent weakness, they say, resides in the reality that frequently the only witness to the crime is the wife. Suppose the wife changes her mind or is unwilling to testify against her violent husband by the time the trial date arrives? Numerous district attorneys verify this occurrence. If the attorney decides to subpoena the now-unwilling spouse to the stand, it is doubtful that the jury would be convinced by *one* unwilling witness.[42] Thus, many attorneys are reluctant to issue a warrant when they believe the wife will not pursue her original intent.

Nevertheless, if the prosecutor issues a warrant signed by the judge, the crime of spouse assault is categorized by the statutes of the criminal justice system. Actually, these criminal statutes do not define assault offenses, but merely fix penalties, which are determined by the intent that accompanies the assault. To sustain a conviction, there must be actual violence to the extent that it causes physical harm. In other words, the person must be seriously injured before the law is seriously applied.

It is unlikely, anyway, that an assailant will go to prison even if found guilty. Even while awaiting trial, he may be out on bond or personal recognizance. This should not inhibit a wife from prosecuting, since by her action the court will be aware that the woman's husband is dangerous, or potentially so, and will attempt to help correct the person's behavior through counseling.[76]

At times, marriage counseling is a viable alternative when the married partners are both willing and able to work seriously at understanding and correcting the underlying causes of the abusive behavior. Professional counselors have achieved some success in working with these violent marriages in a therapeutic setting; but many counselors believe that the only real solution is divorce. One investigation noted that two-thirds of the couples studied had at some time received counseling related to domestic violence; but few husbands cooperated.[44]

If the counseling sessions fail and the violent attacks continue, then the husband will be arraigned in the District Court. At the arraignment the assailant is brought to the Court and advised by the judge of the charges against him and of his legal rights. If the assailant cannot afford to hire an attorney, then the court appoints a public defender. The judge also sets bail for an amount that will bring the defendant back for the next court appearance.

The preliminary hearing allows the defendant to know the charges and witnesses against him. The victim must be present at the hearing, otherwise the defendant will be released. The prosecutor handling the preliminary hearing is usually not the person who authorized the warrant. The victim can be called as a witness and should be prepared by her attorney for this experience. If the prosecutor can show enough proof that a crime was committed, then the judge will order the defendant to go to trial. The District Court then binds the case over to the Circuit Court.

A person arrested for a felonious assault will probably not be detained for more than 48 hours if he is able to post bond. But a peace bond can be, and is often, issued by the judge or magistrate as a judicial threat to control the future behavior of the assailant. This measure can be effective punitively if the fines are sufficiently heavy to force him into making a behavioral change.

The prosecutor may meet with the defense attorney after the preliminary hearing to discuss the possibility of a plea. The defendant can plead guilty to the crime as charged or to a lesser crime, thereby averting the case from going to court. The prosecutor considers the seriousness of the crime, the strength of the evidence, and the defendant's criminal record. If the prosecutor believes he has a good case, he will not authorize a plea of guilty to a lesser charge.

If the prosecutor accepts the plea offer, the defendant and the attorney take the authorization form to the judge. When the judge is satisfied that the defendant is guilty, the plea is taken and a date is set for sentencing. Plea bargaining can occur any time between the reporting of the crime and the trial date. Plea bargaining doesn't actually substantially change the time of probation or prison, but it does save time, energy and tax dollars. The victim is usually not consulted during plea bargaining.

As the case progresses through the Circuit Court, the wife beater is arraigned again, during which time he hears the formal charges against him and a plea is entered into the record. The defendant may plead guilty, not guilty, "stand mute," or "no contest." If the defendant stands mute, the judge automatically enters a plea of not guilty and asks if the defendant would like a trial by jury. Bail is set again and since it is a different court and judge, the bail may not be the same as that set in district court. Then a trial date is established.

The victim is informed of the court date for the trial. Trial dates can be delayed several times. These delays may be due to overload court dockets or defense attorneys wanting more time to prepare the case. Sometimes defense attorneys request delays hoping to tire the victim and get them to drop the case.

The defendant has a choice of either a bench or jury trial. The prosecutor at this level will probably be different from the one who presented the case at the preliminary hearing. The complaining witness may be called to the stand and questioned several times by the prosecutor and defense attorney. Both attorneys, at the start of the trial, will present their arguments to the jury. At the close of the trial, both attorneys will summarize the trial and argue why they think a jury should render a particular decision. The twelve jurors must decide either the guilt or innocence of a defendant beyond a reasonable doubt. The decision must be unanimous. If the defendant is found guilty, he is sentenced within two weeks; if innocent, he is set free.

The attorney for the victim prepares by carefully ascertaining all the details about the assault: the exact time, what events preceded it, what happened, how long it lasted, and all the other circumstances. Sometimes a victim is intimidated by a defense attorney, therefore she should be well prepared by her attorney and attend another trial to gain experience. But during the preparation as well as during the trial, honesty is the best policy.[76]

To demonstrate vividly the criminal justice

process in wife-battering cases, here is the sequence of events in an unfortunate woman's life as she tried to end her husband's violence against her.

First, she obtained a court injunction forbidding him from bothering or harassing her. Although the injunction was issued April 28, it was not served until July. In fact, the harassed woman's mother, enraged with the inaction, went to the sheriff's office, picked up the injunction and served it herself! When the director of the court services was questioned about the delay, he explained that 12 men handle about 350 out of a 1,000 services a month, which he contends is a good batting average.

The woman had called the Police Department more than 100 times and twice filed complaints against her husband. The Police Chief commented that this woman's problems were more than familiar to his department. He added that the wife wanted the husband arrested for violating the court injunction; what she didn't understand was that the only way this could be done was for her to return to court, prove the violation and obtain another court order. She responded that the police did not recommend or encourage her to sign a criminal complaint because the only result of this action would have been to anger her violent husband.

Subsequently, the wife's brother had a fist fight with her husband. Both were arrested. Charges against her brother were later dropped. The husband pleaded guilty to a misdemeanor;

the sentence was dropped by a municipal judge. As a result of this trial, the wife's family felt that they had been put through a wringer and wrung dry. The husband only gained confidence that he could get away with another assault!

Next, the wife had the Telephone Company place a trace on her line to prove that the husband was making threatening phone calls and she later borrowed a tape recorder from the police to record the calls. One tape recorded the husband saying that, "he was coming over to kill all of you." The police later seemed to have misplaced the tapes.

The wife obtained a second court order—a bench warrant—for the husband's arrest because he failed to show up for a court hearing to explain why he did not obey the injunction. She went before the City Council to complain that the police were not giving her any help with the husband's violent threats and attacks.

In trying to secure justice for this woman, her family wrote the State Governor, her Congressman and the Department of Corrections asking, "Where can a person get help with something like this problem?"

Finally, a Circuit Judge issued a bench warrant a week after the husband failed to show up at a court hearing to explain why he ignored the injunction to stop harassing his wife and her family. *The arrest was not made until the husband attacked his wife. The police who arrested him did so because he was wanted by the circuit court.* The detective who handled the assault case commented that the wife was scared to death, absolutely terrified of her husband.[59]

These involved episodes indicate the depressing combination of social and legal indifference which make it extremely difficult for a wife to escape from an intolerable situation. The police and the courts display an inordinate reluctance to prosecute a husband. The hassles, the time consumed and the anguish suffered by battered women to obtain justice, cause one to wonder why any pursue it at all!

One route available for women to redress grievances is the criminal law and courts; another is the civil law and courts.

The principle means available in the area of civil law and the courts is divorce. One study indicates that two-thirds of the couples who experienced physical violence had separated at some time and almost half are now divorced or are in the process of divorce.[44] Many professionals who work in the field of domestic violence believe the most effective remedy is divorce, although many also add that it does not prevent an ex-husband from returning and beating up his ex-wife.

Another study indicates that even with divorce the problem remains unsolved because the husband continues his assaults during visitations with the children. But at times divorce is the woman's only effective remedy to correct her man's violent attacks. Moreover, the wife must be willing in a divorce proceeding legally to do battle through an attorney for property rights, support and sometimes even for custody of the children.[44]

During a divorce proceeding, every battered woman should obtain a restraining order as part of the marriage settlement.[76] The restraining order's aim is to restrict the assailant from further assaults on his wife. It orders the assailant to 'desist and refrain from beating, annoying, molesting, physically abusing, or otherwise interfering with the personal liberty of the other" during the divorce proceedings, usually 6 to 18 months or longer.[11]

This procedure, unfortunately, is time-consuming, monetarily costly and, due to the discretionary powers of the judge, can result in his merely giving *a warning* to the assailant. In spite of these qualifications, a wife in the midst of a divorce proceeding should obtain such an order. At times, policemen who follow a district attorney's orders will not arrest a husband who is clearly in violation of a civil restraining order (which is a misdemeanor in itself), but will tell the wife to call her attorney. This reluctance to arrest a spouse when he is behaving unlawfully is not due to any difficulties in the interpretation of court orders, but is often based on the belief that battered women do not pursue prosecution. There also exists a political and criminal justice tradition in domestic cases of discrimination against women.[42]

In New York, a restraining order can be sought easily and, if the husband violates the conditions of the order, he can be arrested and sentenced up to six months in jail. When enforced, this type of order can be effective. Since during the divorce proceedings it is very hard to evict a man from his home, the woman frequently finds herself trapped within the four walls of the home with a bully who mistreats her cruelly at will. Even though this order is not frequently effective in restricting a husband's violent behavior, a super-restraining order should always be demanded by an attorney for a battered woman and be included in a final divorce settlement.

Two women in northern Virginia struggled to obtain justice and peace within the court system. These are their tragic and frightening experiences.

At times, it is not the police nor the district attorney nor the judge who apparently ignore a woman's pleas, but the very person she hires, a person supposedly contracted to obtain justice for her—her attorney. These two women played tennis at the same club, shared mutual friends and car pools, lived in adjoining Fairfax County subdivisions and appeared to their friends as contented wives of retired high-ranking Army officers.

They never shared notes on a common problem: their husbands beat them violently and they were never able to attain effective protection from further assaults despite repeated desperate efforts. Only after they decided to take independent legal action against their husbands—and had become bitterly frustrated by mistreatment from police, magistrates and lawyers—did they confide in each other. Both complained that they found no place offering them protection, no reasonably priced legal advice, or even anyone to talk with. Both claimed they had been humiliated by police officers and magistrates, who refused to take their pleas seriously, and that they had been over-charged by a series of lawyers.

The first lady, Mrs. M. continues to this day to receive threats on her life from her husband who has tried to beat or strangle her several times, including once in front of her mother-in-law.

Mrs. M. said her husband began to beat her when he decided to retire from the Army as a Colonel and announced that he was going to marry a 19-year old lifeguard. When the girl had second thoughts and backed out of the marriage, he began to beat his wife. He swung from chandeliers, threw things at her and hit her. Yet if anyone else entered the room, he would change into a well-mannered, meek person. He even inflicted scratches on himself, claiming that his wife did it.

She left home, but could find no place to live. She moved from one home to another with her 9-year old son. Finally, she found a town house to rent, but this did not end the beatings. One day she returned to the family house and found most of the 200 and 300-year old antiques missing. Her husband, with blurry eyes, said that he was going to kill her. He said that the court would find him insane; he would spend a year in a mental institution and then be free. Six more assaults occurred during the next nine months, one in which she was thrown down a flight of stairs, injuring her back and legs. A Fairfax County judge found him guilty of assault and forced entry, fined him $500 and a suspended 30 day jail sentence.

She testified that her first lawyer lied to her, failed to see that a restraining order was enforced and bargained away her rights. Her present lawyer told her to take a $10,000 divorce settlement (which is far below the amount she should actually receive), because of the errors her first lawyer made.

The second woman, Mrs. B., said in a court deposition that her husband, a West Point graduate and then an up-and-coming Army officer, began beating her soon after the marriage. He began to drink, became intoxicated, and then physically abused her. In one drunken rage, she was attacked by her husband with his military academy sword, cutting her arm so badly that it took 17 stitches to close the wound. He also turned on a friend who tried to break up the fight. The friend, a fellow officer, reported the incident and her husband was hospitalized for alcoholism. Mrs. B. commented that this particular incident probably cost her husband his generalship.

When he retired as a full colonel, he couldn't find work and began to drink excessively. Yet whenever she mentioned his excessive drinking to him, he would fly into a rage. The final straw was when he accused her of nipping his liquor— his liquor bill that year was $1700—and beat her savagely against the kitchen sink. She decided it was the last time she would permit that to happen to her.

Mrs. B. claims she was billed $3000 for two brief court appearances, one routine legal brief, and a series of itemized phone calls.

Both women reserve their greatest outrage for lawyers, who they claim treated them arrogantly, overcharged them, misled and misrepresented them in several instances and were difficult to contact at different moments.[69]

Some districts have established family bureaus as auxiliaries to aid the criminal justice system. The aims and objectives of these family bureaus are certainly well-intentioned, but they often fall far short of the mark.

One such bureau was set up in San Francisco and received most of its referrals from the San Francisco District Attorney's Office. No California statute authorizes this bureau, which consists of four investigators, none of whom are trained lawyers or psychologists. As soon as a family or quasi-family relationship is involved in the complaint, it is referred to this Family Bureau. The Bureau applies its procedures of investigation, referral, counseling and quasi-adjudication to the problem with the result that the vast majority of *the cases never reach the offices of the assistant district attorney or the district attorney, even though the wife may have desired to press charges.*

During the years 1969-70, the Family Bureau handled 10,234 cases; of these cases 2,502 were referred to outside agencies with no follow-up; and only 1,615 cases resulted in an informal citation hearing held by the Family Bureau itself. In 1973, the Family Bureau received over 5000 calls; only *eight* of these cases led to complaint and prosecution by the district attorney's office. Such facts offer some idea of *the vast number of family disputes that are dismissed from the criminal justice system and all but officially ignored.*

If the battered woman insists that some action be taken, and if there is evidence that the injuries are severe and a history of violence exists between the partners, then a citation hearing will be scheduled. The Family Bureau's first step is to send the accused a polite note to attend. If he refuses, a second strongly worded note is sent which mentions that a warrant for his arrest will be issued if he does not attend the hearing. Usually this second note is an empty threat because seldom does arrest follow a failure to appear at a citation hearing. If the accused husband does attend the citation hearing, any solution reached is useless to the beaten wife because it is not legally binding. Once home again with her husband, she is at his mercy, dependent upon his discretion to beat or not to beat her.

The district attorney's office gives unlimited discretion to the Family Bureau in dismissing wife-beating cases, but is very reluctant to concur when the discretion is exercised in favor of prosecution. The flip side of the coin—prosecution—demands severe requirements; the woman must preferably have two witnesses to the beating, a police report should be on file, the injuries must be severe, the woman must be aggressive in wanting to pursue the matter, and the offender must be a repeater. If these conditions are present, then the Family Bureau investigator will discuss the case, not with the district attorney, but with a police investigator.

Given these stringent conditions preceding a warrant, it is a wonder that even eight warrants were issued in 1973! It is even more remarkable that the battered women received the blame for not following through when the conditions are so difficult to meet. One woman was so frustrated by the Family Bureau procedures that she asked, "What do I have to do to get him arrested, wait 'till he kills me?"[42]

6. SPREADING CANCER

Although the battered wife's violent experiences are truly harrowing and denigrating, consider the serious spin offs onto the children. Imagine a youngster witnessing his father aggressively and violently attacking his mother. What a traumatic impact these dreadful scenes must necessarily have on the malleable and impressionable young person! Then carrying the scene further on to what frequently occurs in this situation, imagine what confusion and bitterness must rise up in a youngster who in turn, after witnessing a brutal beating visited on someone he loves, becomes himself the brunt of a senseless and shameless beating.

To place in perspective the violent physical punishment inflicted on American children within the home, we have to examine some salient characteristics in the history of child abuse.

American culture's level of abusive parental behavior against children is deplorably high but the phenomenon itself has existed in cultures and societies for centuries. At times, physical punishment was judged necessary to instill education, placate the gods, discipline children, or even drive evil spirits out of the child.[72] As recently as the last century did church workers through the American Society for the Prevention of Cruelty to Animals (ASPCA) have a child removed from her parents on the grounds that she was a member of the animal kingdom and therefore her case could be included under the laws of cruelty to animals!

Through the indefatigable efforts of reformers in this country a "Children's Charter" was adopted, which promised full-time public welfare services for the protection of children from abuse, neglect, exploitation or moral hazard. But only in the last couple of decades in this country has the battered child syndrome received the attention and friends it deserves to combat and change the situation of these unfortunate children.[26]

The family may teach, approve and condone the use of violence and this conditions family members to interact violently. If a husband and father frequently or even occasionally resorts to violence to control a family situation, then this behavior is a powerful indicator that violence is acceptable. If the father of a family places a high priority on the value of force and abuse as a means for settling disputes, then the children catch this same attitude.

A coordinator of the Dade County, Florida Task Force on Battered Women recalled an 8-year old who threatened that if his mother didn't do as he demanded, "I'll tell Daddy to beat you up."[100] This last instance also indicates that a husband's attack against the wife often occurs in the presence of the children, but rarely in the presence of other persons.[44] When violence is used and it attains its desired effect, this reinforcement produces an even greater impetus towards more violence. Parents who use physical punishment or heap violent abuse on one another provide their children with violent models. Children learn by imitation. If they learn that adults control their situations by means of violence, it is likely they will resort to the same means of control. Violence becomes acceptable.[20, 30, 88, 91]

A Kalamazoo study indicates the validity of this viewpoint: fully two-fifths of the abusive husbands had been abused as children. Likewise, in one-third of the cases for which child abuse information was available, the assaulter was also said to abuse his children as well as his wife.[44] A study of 100 wife-battering cases showed that in 54 of the cases, the violence had spilled over onto the children, and many women gave this as a reason for leaving their husbands and homes. Fifty-one women of those 100 interviewed claimed that they had knowledge that their husbands had been exposed to family violence in childhood.[27]

Violent attitudes emerged after the Kent State tragedy; many parents bitterly commented that long-haired hippies deserved to be shot even if they were their own children. Among the most verbally violent were many women who displayed a depth of bitterness and an intensity of rejection for these young persons that apparently could easily be carried over into actual physically abusive behavior against their own young children.[56]

There seems to be a direct correlation between wives who are battered and women who batter their children. Researchers who study child abuse find that children are killed more often by their mothers than by their fathers. One study reported that the ratio was 88 to 43 with mothers killing their children more often than fathers.[75] Another study, revealed that in ten cases of child abuse, seven abusers were women.[30]

In a further 57 cases of child abuse, the mother was the abuser 50 times.[85] Child abuse and wife assault are intimately connected. The 100 women surveyed, who were mentioned above, have 315 children. It is distressing to realize how many persons are seriously scarred by beatings.[27] Since frequently battered children grow up to be battering parents, it is a sobering thought to analyze the geometric progression built-in to this syndrome.

It is estimated that as many as two million children each year in the U.S. are victims of a form of familial violence called child abuse. The number could reach even as many as 10 million abused children annually according to the definition of child abuse used.[33,36] Once this vicious cycle begins, it seems to perpetuate itself from one generation of assaulters to another. Each generation of children learns that violence is acceptable and necessary to control others in their life-space.

Endeavoring to learn the early life experiences of 51 men convicted of murder, a researcher interviewed these men, their relatives and friends in New England during the years 1956-1959. A control group of 51 men who were the nearest in-age brother to each murderer, and who had not committed a murder, was used as a measure for the number and severity of beatings received as a child. The mothers of the murderers beat them more often and more severely than their nearest-age-brother. The fathers interviewed also admitted that they frequently beat their son who eventually committed murder.[65]

The predominant form of violence in a family is corporal punishment of children by parents. In the U.S. and England, according to various studies, between 84% and 97% of all parents use physical punishment at some point in the child's life.[91, 92] Nor do these figures signify that corporal punishment is relegated to the childhood years, during which time parental authority is maintained.

One study reported that half of the students in the sample from three different regions of the U.S., who were beaten or were threatened with a beating, were seniors in high school.[87]

Corporal punishment is used by parents to control their children's behavior even into late adolescence. Violence becomes a teacher and a conditioner as well as an acceptable form of behavior for the parents to use against their children, even though it usually does not improve the child's behavior.

This is not to say that a child does not need a spanking from time to time to help him learn acceptable behavior. At times, a child who at three-years-old bolts into the street may need a spanking to teach him not to practise this self-injuring behavior. But this is a far cry from abuse or physical violence visited on a child or adolescent for small behavioral flaws or for just being present when either parent has flown into a rage. Although some authorities condone the use of violence by parents to discipline recalcitrant children, it usually boomerangs.[20]

Physical violence used against youths usually increases their own aggressive tendencies. Violence begets violence. Physical punishment has not only the tendency to increase aggressive acts in the child's life-space but also to produce a child who is relatively low in internalized moral standards and self-direction.[89] These last two flaws in personality development apparently are present in many wife-beaters. Such persons learn these behaviors very early in life and by continuous reinforcement form violence-prone characters.

Some fathers of families, particularly when their children are males, place a high priority on teaching their sons toughness and the skills necessary to win a street fight. This is not to claim that a knowledge of self defense tactics is unimportant if correctly and prudently taught. But too often these fathers who teach their sons violent and aggressive skills and behavior lack a close and supportive relationship with them and are equipping them with skills that will be used destructively against those who are closest to the male as an adult. Such a father is providing a sure formula for a child's later violent behavior against those whom he feels thwart him.

Erin Pizzy, the foundress of shelters for battered women in England, comments that a man who batters is a child who was battered and whom nobody helped. These men were either beaten as children or watched their mothers being beaten.[101] The physically abused child usually is scarred psychologically, often carrying these scars into adulthood to become a violent parent. Those children who watch their mothers being beaten also suffer severe internal pain.

Viewing these physically violent scenes, children respond in varying ways. Some break out in severe cases of acne. Some blame themselves for parental problems. Others keep an intact record of the beatings on a pad hoping that this behavior will produce some magical effect of cessation. After a fatiguing night of witnessing their mothers abused, they can't drag themselves to school the next day or are just neglected and do what they please.

These children are also often used as pawns for blackmailing or as hostages for a reconciliation.[98] It is no wonder that, once they are grown up, they find it so difficult to make a viable marriage. Children in homes where wife-battering occurs display varying degrees of pathology. Usually the girls tend to be passive and withdrawn while the boys tend to be aggressive and destructive.[101]

Such pathological children develop this unsteady emotional balance from their parents' pathological behavior. Developmental stresses in them are magnified by discord within the family. A child receives distorted images in a matrix of chronic marital discord. As the child reaches out for love, he is rebuffed with physical abuse and the parents' emotional responses are untrue sounding boards. As a result, the child's normal integration of aggressive tendencies into his personality cannot be achieved.

Frequently, mothers who are battered become tense and neurotic, attitudes which are communicated to their children. These "contagion" effects were noted during the London blitz, when tense mothers communicated their anxiety to their children, who, in turn displayed neurotic symptoms, whereas relaxed mothers did not unduly disturb their children.[19] Besides these effects, disturbed marital relationships cause the offspring of these marriages to prolong the period of normal dependence and to form "clinging" relationships with their mothers.

Apparently, wife-battering is directly related to child-abuse. Some men batter both their wives and their children, others batter their wives in the presence of their children. Both teach their children that violence is an appropriate way of controlling a frustrating situation. Some women abuse their children as a consequence of being beaten by their husbands or out of a sense of personal frustration. The end result of all this is that children are battered and this prepares them to become violent and battering adults. The physical and psychological scars a child receives as a consequence of parental violence are carried into adulthood to perpetuate the disaster.

7. WHAT CAN BE DONE

Now more than ever is the acceptable time to lessen or significantly lower heart-rendering episodes of beatings and family violence, because the problem—once it is out in the open—can be effectively met with concrete proposals and actions. What are some of these?

EACH OF US is called upon to change his attitudes. Each of us, in his or her own way, can influence society's patterns of behavior. If our attitudes about wife-beating are that the problem is nonexistent or merely a spat between a husband and wife which we consequently view as a domestic dispute without any meaning for us, it is time we tried to evaluate seriously this destructive behavior.

If we believe that a husband can slap or kick

his wife around from time to time just as we may kick a folding chair to open or close it, then we have to reflect seriously on the real social maladies that follow in the wake of wife-beating. Each of us, by being responsible and responsive to this problem, can change commonly accepted beliefs.

THE MEDIA PEOPLE—newspapers, magazines, television, radio, and all other modern technological attitude-formers and shapers—should sensitize themselves to this problem and take a firm stand that domestic violence and specifically wife-beating will be depicted as a destructive and denigrating behavior. When domestic violence is enacted on television the main message ought to be that it is not all right to beat a woman and that it is usually not the woman's fault who is beaten.

ANOTHER REMEDY at our disposal is to form small consciousness-raising groups in our local churches and temples as well as in other community agencies. These groups allow husbands and wives the freedom to talk out the problems associated with living in a family where a partner resorts to violence to resolve tensions and frustrations. They will allow the person the opportunity to clarify his perspectives and seek the necessary help before it is too late.

WOMEN SHOULD BE ENCOURAGED to enroll in courses that teach the skills associated with the martial arts. This remedy is not suggested as a means to meet violence with violence. It is not an attempt to equip women with skills to enable them to do battle with men. But a working knowledge of karate will help a woman to defend herself if the need arises.

This suggestion does not envision the scenario of a woman attending classes for several years so as to be able to fight back against a battering mate. A woman who becomes adept in karate still remains a target for an irate male who can beat her with a chair or a baseball bat. Her acquired skills will simply allow her to fend off a first attack and not become a weak, convenient target for his abuse. Furthermore, these classes can aid her to be more self-disciplined, more self-confident and generally more able physically to protect herself.

COMMUNITY RESOURCES are frequently not mobilized to deal with the problems of wife assaulters. The resources available are not energized to meet this crisis. The battered woman finds herself caught tightly in a double bind: if she seeks help, it is often ineffective in solving the problem; if she doesn't seek help, the batterings continue. Whether she acts or not, her problem is not relieved.

Many professional people also blame the battered woman for remaining in the situation. The common professional attitude is that if a battered spouse remains in the home, then in some way she must be satisfying a sick need to be beaten. For example, a district attorney who wants a show of good faith by insisting that the woman initiate divorce proceedings is really blaming her if she wants to remain married.

RESOURCE SERVICES ought to be formed to assist families who are involved in wife assault situations. Personnel who work in professional agencies need to be educated in effective procedures to resolve this problem. In fact, communities in general should be educated concerning this dire social need and assisted in learning what individuals can do to alleviate the battered wife's anguish.

TO OVERCOME community apathy and incompetency in dealing with the wife assault problem, communities ought to form a "Concerned Citizens Group" to determine effective ways of dealing with it. The make-up of the citizens group should include legal persons, i.e. staff from the prosecuting attorney's office, legal aid personnel, private attorneys, office personnel, and family court judges.

It should also be composed of health service representatives, police department representatives, personnel from counseling agencies, both marriage and alcoholic treatment centers, as well as physicians, psychiatrists, psychologists, and private citizens who can appropriately contribute to solve this problem.[44] The purposes and procedures of a concerned citizens group ought to aim at outlining multiple ways and means to deal effectively with the problem. The following areas are suggestions to aid a community to realize its goals:

An in-depth research study should be inaugurated to learn how to better treat and solve the problem of wife assault.

The personnel who gather the data for this research study ought to include the resource persons cited above because they frequently possess the knowledge, experience and qualifications to offer concrete and legitimate insights to solve the battered wife problem.

The citizens group members should determine methods of establishing social indicators to obtain a more accurate report of incidence.

THE COOPERATION OF THE LOCAL POLICE department ought to be sought to insure that hard, contemporary data is collected and classified.

They should attempt to find new legal alternatives, rather than limiting wives to the often ineffective peace bonds and restraining orders.

One example of a possible new legal alternative would be a writ of mandamus, which is an equitable action traditionally brought to compel an officer, board, or court to exercise its discretion when it refuses to act at all. If the police are not enforcing the laws in regard to family violence perpetrated against women, then the discriminatory effect of their behavior is evident. By means of the act of mandamus, the police can be forced to exercise this mandate to apply the law in wife assault instances.[42]

A feasability study ought to be done to assess the possibility of making available an assistant prosecutor on weekends to offer battered women the opportunity to arrest their physically violent husbands. If domestic violence occurs on a Friday or Saturday night, which is frequently the case, then it becomes an intolerable home situation to expect a wife to remain in the home with this volatile man until Monday morning when the prosecutor's office is open for service. If an arrest is called for, then it should be made at the time of the violence.

Although Married Woman's Acts began to be passed by individual state legislatures following the Civil War until today, and although every State possesses such acts, they still do not immediately render the husband liable to suit for striking his wife. Even today the wife is severely limited to criminal law or divorce to halt an abusive husband's acts. Criminal law is difficult to invoke, as a previous chapter indicated, and often ineffective, while divorce is an extreme step. Even though the law is applied unevenly and often ambiguously, *a husband has no right to use physical punishment against his wife.*[10]

Citizen groups ought to use moral suasion to ensure that the courts apply the law to correct abusive husbands acts. They should also work to improve linkages between existing structures; attorneys frequently interpret the law differently, so a valuable step would be to form a consensus about the meaning of the law and the legal implications of certain actions.

For example, in the case of a woman who leaves the children or home to separate from an intolerable physically violent husband, the legal implications should be clarified.

Another valuable assistance would be in enlisting the help of paralegal professionals who could gather the necessary information and process it rather than consuming the time and effort of practicing attorneys.

The members of the concerned citizens group should examine new roles for the police in dealing with "domestic muggings." Most of the activity of a police officer in contemporary American society consists of interpersonal services. These services often demand that the police officer be skillful in arbitration, mediation and advisement.

It has been estimated that approximately 90% of a police officer's daily activity entails such interpersonal services. Yet a police officer's job preparation seldom includes the training necessary to foster interpersonal skills and effective interventional methods. The police model is frequently based on an outmoded paradigm of a pistol toting repressor of violence who chases and apprehends crooks. His real role is more often to arbitrate, mediate and advise.

Some suggestions in this area are that the police should write out their policies regarding domestic dispute intervention and allow the public to review them. Recently, after lengthy discussions, the San Francisco Police Commission permitted public hearings to receive responsible insights from lay and professional persons regarding the recently published Police Manual of General Procedures and Manual for Rules for the San Francisco Police Department. This police procedure insured the public's interest and support plus a well-thought out manual.42

Another suggestion is that domestic violence calls should be given an "A" or "B" priority and not be relegated to a "C" level because of the real threat of physical injury to the woman.

An idea worth repeating, is that when a battered woman phones the police she merely informs them that a *man* is about to or has physically attacked her. She should not use the word *husband* because some police departments ignore domestic violence calls.

The police should respond promptly to a domestic dispute call, and when they encounter violence at the scene of a domestic mugging, they should make an arrest. They should also inform a woman of her right to make a citizen's arrest. When violence is not a threat, then the police ought to refer the couple to an appropriate social agency.

All police officers should be trained in domestic intervention techniques. This training would allow the police to interfere effectively and reduce the number of tragic incidents of police injury.

Specially trained mobile crises teams could be formed to respond to police calls involving domestic violence. These crises teams would attempt to explain to husbands alternate ways of dealing with domestic tension other than beating their wives.

Here is one practical example of what can be done: a program in police family crisis intervention was designed and instituted by the New York City Police Department to provide a unique service to a West Harlem community of about 85,000 people. An intensive month-long preparatory program sensitized the policemen to their own values about human behavior in general and about disrupted families in particular.

When their training was completed, these policemen answered all domestic violence calls within the area of the precinct. Not one homicide was reported in 22 months in any family that the team had visited previously, since it began to operate in the 30th precinct. They also were able to refer a number of family dispute cases to appropriate social and mental health agencies instead of routing them all through the Family Court which is the usual police procedure. The unit has become a permanent effective innovation in the precinct.

The police techniques in this unit include the separation of the disputants to neutralize potential violence. Then each officer engages in a conversation with one of the disputants with as much privacy as possible. Some officers in the unit then switch disputants and carry on a conversation with the other partner. This is followed by a four-way group discussion. Other officers, after their private chats with the disputants, take the position of their client and with the disputants watching, often in surprised awe, two officers heatedly argue the case. This last technique apparently adds sufficient objectivity to the situation for the disputants to allow a meaningful dialogue to follow.[2]

An added note on the formation of a family crisis intervention team, which ought to add a valuable dimension to the make-up of the team, is to include police women. This female dimension will add a conciliatory and sensitive feminine influence to the usually highly emotional and aggressive family situation.

When an effective family intervention police team operates in a neighborhood, the word travels through the neighborhood grapevine that this team is all right and can be trusted.

Police departments ought also to gather specific data on the number of domestic violence calls, time-lapses in response, the number of arrests made, and the number of repeat calls, serious injuries and homicides involved in these types of interventions.

To return to citizens' group activity, they should also investigate legislative reforms to alleviate the battered wife syndrome. Such reform may not achieve its goal because it is a long arduous task to write and enact new laws which in fact may not be really necessary, so it seems that the primary task in the legislative area ought to be the enforcement of laws already on the books. Nevertheless, a statute could be added to the civil law which clearly states that when serious injury results as a consequence of a public employee's abuse of discretion—police officer, assistant district attorney, etc.—then that employee is accountable to the society by law.

The professionals who comprise the citizens group could also package a help-yourself kit for battered women. This would be a guide for assaulted women to assist the victims of domestic violence take the necessary steps to stand firm against further violent acts.

The group should recommend and help initiate re-education programs for the personnel of social service agencies to help them deal more effectively with this problem. Although most marriage counselors sincerely strive to salvage marriages when they can, it is extremely difficult to heal the wounds caused by a physically violent spouse. Yet, by means of programs to better their skills, the counselors can identify the problem and attempt to offer the atmosphere and support for an open and healthy confrontation between the spouses.

Frequently the only effective resolution of these cases is a "good dose of distance" between the spouses. Geographically, at least temporarily, they need distance between themselves. This temporary separation may lead to divorce, but it may be the only healthy solution for the fighting couple. Not that marriage counseling or the counseling of spouses in a violent marriage should aim at a divorce. The point is that this resolution, a times, is the only sane one.

Too often the advice given to a wife is, "You have a marital home; go home." The courts often advise women to try to forgive and forget and remake the marriage. The common attitude of judges is that the assailant needs a threat and he will change. They tend "to wag a finger" at the assailant and send him home with a lecture, which the wife assaulter can readily ignore at his whim.

Another common attitude of both judges and probation officers who refer wife-batterers to a marital counseling agency is that there must be something wrong with a man who would beat his wife, especially when he has a good job, a nice home, children, and an outwardly stable family. The inference is that he is probably mentally unbalanced and therefore should be pitied rather than punished. *This is usually not the effective way to treat wife-beaters and only paves the way for repeated violence.*

A DEFINITE NEED EXISTS to develop innovative court procedures in handling effectively the wife-battering problem. One such program has been initiated by a City Court judge in Hammond, Indiana, to check the rising recidivism rate of husbands who beat their wives. He appoints the battered wives as probation officers for their violence-prone husbands! If the family wants to stay together as a unit, then the judge assigns the wife as an officer of the court. This assures the wife speedy and effective intervention if her husband beats her, because she can phone the judge at home or at the court to complain.

In this situation, the wife receives immediate action, whereas previously six to eight weeks might elapse before appropriate action was taken. As soon as the judge receives the wife's phone message, he can revoke the husband's probation and immediately notify the police to arrest him. He may also impose a jail sentence on the husband that may be served on weekends so as not to disrupt the family and this procedure also allows the husband to keep his weekday job. The husband must attend psychological counseling with the proviso that if he fails to attend, his probation is revoked and he goes to jail.

Since this program is less than a year old and since probation usually extends from six months to a year, it is not time-tested. It can be said that thus far, there have been no beatings of court appointed "probation officer" wives. Only those wives are appointed as probation officers whom the court judges will not abuse their special status.

COUNSELORS TO whom wife batterers are

referred must have the necessary expertise to explore and confront the violent husband's behavior and so effect personal change. Counselors can also become advocates to insure proper protection and to help victims of husband assault.

Frequently, other professional mental health workers, i.e. psychiatrists and psychologists, tend to operate from the principle of collusion. This principle, although often not overtly expressed, is that if the woman puts up with her spouse's violent behavior, she needs and wants the violence. Not only do these professionals need to revise this principle, but they also need to study trends in effective treatment and so be better equipped to contribute to the treatment and prevention of violent domestic behavior.

A community based citizens group can cull the best from the already existing counseling centers to aid assaulted women. One such crisis center is called *Abused Women's Aid in Crisis* (*AWAIC*), founded in New York City. In New York in 1962, the legislature transferred jurisdiction over family offenders from the criminal courts to the Family Court, a civil bench. Wife assault cases were taken out of the criminal court and transferred to the civil court because so many women frequently were afraid to prosecute.

The personnel of AWAIC have evaluated this fear that often exists in the wife and have attempted to offer some practical ways of reaching out to these victims. They recognize that even a threat to commit domestic violence should be taken seriously because in 78.7% of all cases of physical violence, a threat had preceded the violence. AWAIC offers hotline counseling, group and individual support programs, evening outreach meetings, a national clearing house for information and referrals, training programs, and legal advice.

This last service is frequently neglected, which means that women who need legal advice often find themselves scraping funds together from family and friends or spending their meager savings to receive the proper legal help. Reasonably priced emergency legal advice ought to be a necessary component of every crisis center. AWAIC opened in February of 1975 and approximately a year later more than a thousand cases from the tri-state area benefited from the center's services. A woman recently wrote AWAIC,

"Had there been someone years ago to listen to me, to advise me of my rights, of my alternative, I might have avoided a tragedy in my life—my son wouldn't now need psychiatric care—and probably, my husband would have sought help."

Hotlines for help truly aid battered women to sort out their confused thoughts and feelings. They give these women an opportunity to choose the appropriate alternative to remaining in a steadily deteriorating situation.

AWAIC's long term goal is to begin a shelter for these women and their children. Although a shelter in every city may be a band-aid response to a social malady that needs massive surgery, shelters should be provided for women who are

103

unable to remain at home. City governments cannot, certainly, permit their efforts to stop at establishing shelters. People in general, and the entire criminal justice system in particular, need to recognize the extent of the problem and take appropriate remedies to solve it.

Yet, one feature that apparently contributes to intra-family violence is the lack of places to which an abused wife can escape and avoid her abusive husband. Relatively minor altercations can escalate into major fist-fights with severe injuries to the woman unless she can seek refuge in a shelter. It is extremely difficult to salvage a marriage where violence has occurred repeatedly.

A battered woman should try to locate a shelter in her area or some peaceful place where she can sift through her life and make a reasonable decision about her future. These "de-escalation stations" offer emotional support, help women to collect their wits and aid them to think about starting anew as a single-parent family.

Shelters are necessary because family and friends frequently do not reach out to these women with an offer of help. The Good Samaritan theory that an abused woman often receives help from her family and friends is usually not true. Some persons who might give aid think they may be legally liable for interfering in a domestic dispute, and others do not help because they fear the assailant may turn on them because they are helping his wife. For these reasons, shelters are frequently the only safe havens for assaulted wives.

There are various shelters which have been established and are effectively helping abused women. One such shelter is Haven House in Los Angeles, California, which offers women and their children a refuge as well as providing comfort and counsel for up to 30 days. When filled, this house can handle 11 women and 25 children. Significantly, it's full all the time.

The Victims Information Bureau of Suffolk County, New York, houses wives in clusters of apartments. These women pay for the lodgings on a sliding scale according to their resources —from nothing up to their full share of rent. Since the Bureau's opening six months ago, about 1,100 women have sought its help. This statistic alone indicates the dire need for such shelters in this area. It is no wonder that the Center for Women's Policy Studies, a feminist organization in Washington, D.C., reports that at least 28 shelters are in the planning stages or have been opened recently across the country.

The Women's Transitional Living Center (WT LC) in Fullerton, California, was established in January of 1976 by many interested women who believed that there was a great need for a shelter. This Orange County Shelter can house for 30 days 18 people who are victims of husband abuse. Many women who arrive at this shelter have shattered self-concepts. The shelter's personnel have restored a number of them to normal life-styles and they have become active,

105

healthy contributors in the community.

Another shelter is being established by Las Casas de Las Madres Coalition in San Francisco, California, to provide social services to the predominantly Spanish-surnamed battered women of the area. The director, Mama O'Shea, was surprised to learn how many supposedly religious men who neither drink nor smoke and who attend church regularly beat their wives.[100]

Rainbow Retreat, Inc. located in Phoenix, Arizona, is a crisis, residential treatment facility for the physically and/or emotionally abused female non-alcoholic spouse. In addition, they provide outpatient service which provides counseling and group therapy for the entire family as well as a 24 hour telephone service to families in an alcoholic crisis. This one-story, single family residence houses 13 women and children daily, 24 hours a day, 7 days a week.

Residents have arrived from the state of Arizona as well as California, New Mexico, Chicago and even as far east as New Jersey seeking their services. This should alert other States of the dire need for such shelters and services. Through Rainbow's multi-faceted program which includes alcohol abuse education, the staff has influenced 64% of the alcohol abusers through their spouses to seek treatment.

The project was founded November 1, 1973, and was the first model emergency shelter in the nation to provide residential care for the abused spouse of the problem drinker. Although Rainbow Retreat maintains that alcohol abuse accounts for many of the beatings a woman may receive, its personnel also recognizes the need to probe deeper into the psychological causes for a husband's abusive behavior.

To understand more fully the help afforded an abused woman at Rainbow, we shall walk briefly in the footsteps of a woman once she enlists the facility's help. Upon arriving, she is given a loving, supportive and caring atmosphere. She is allowed a 24 hour emotional venting and rest period during which time she gets the feelings off her chest and out in the open concerning her spouse's abusive behavior.

After this phase a concentrated and serious effort is made to educate her in her participation in the progression of the family problem. The five objectives of this phase in Rainbow's program are to remove the isolative feelings of the woman, to make her aware of how she may be contributing to the problem, to educate her in alternative behaviors in coping with the problem, to prevent the continuance of her past self-defeating behaviors and to intervene with help for her spouse.

The new arrival at Rainbow is assigned duties. She participates in lectures. Every day she has an hour of personal counseling and she participates in group and rap sessions in learning to deal with herself. She also attends self-improvement classes which are therapeutic in content as well as art and exercise therapy classes. She is given job training with a view of eventual job placement.

The non-resident woman is offered the same program but she resides outside of the facility.[74] Rainbow's multi-faceted program has helped many families to function at a marked level of improvement and seems to offer a model for other shelters to imitate.

Our Canadian neighbors have also recognized the dire need for shelters to house battered women. One such shelter has been established in Ottawa on a slightly run-down street in a semi-detached house and is called Interval House. Furnished with donated items, the house is bright and clean. Children's artwork decorates the walls along with posters that speak of dreams and visions. Women who come here are given a chance to sort out their lives which frequently have histories of beatings.

The facility is funded by a Local Initiative Program (LIP) and was established as a result of a survey sponsored by the Secretary of the State Department which revealed that in any given month approximately 100 women could use a place like Interval House.[17]

This whole concept of establishing shelters for battered women was pioneered by an English-woman, Erin Pizzy. Since her initial efforts, shelters now house women in the environs of London and number about 17.

A policeman's wife may appear on a shelter doorstep with six broken ribs, burns on her thighs from boiling water and bruises all over her face. A 19-year-old with a ruptured gall bladder arrives, having been kicked and slashed. A woman collapses on the doorstep: she has been raped at knifepoint by her husband in front of her three sons. These are daily scenes occurring at Chiswick Women's Aid and the various houses established by Erin Pizzy to aid these women.[101]

An alternative to actually founding shelters is the innovative plan inaugurated in Ann Arbor, Michigan, which has helped to solve the problem of a refuge for women. Private families volunteer their homes for a maximum of three days and nights to these women and their children to afford them the opportunity to escape the beatings, find an apartment, begin legal procedures and decide about their futures.[100]

Refuges for battered women can reduce significantly the beatings that they suffer. On the other hand, the lack of shelters is a feature that actually contributes to intra-family violence because a woman and her children are locked into a husband's violently abusive behaviors. Without a safe haven, relatively minor altercations can escalate into major beatings with severe injuries to the wife and the children.

It is never too late to enact the legal, law

enforcement, psychological and social remedies mentioned in this chapter. And it is not too soon. If our society and its institutional structures are to remain strong and integral, families must be havens of love and gentleness.

Husbands and wives have to encounter one another with love and respect through daily dialoguing. Masks which cover a husband and wife's genuine feelings and ideas have to be put aside and each person must attempt to accept the other with understanding. The time-honored truth that the greatest gift husbands and wives can give their children is the love they give to each other is now more than ever valid. The friendship that husbands and wives create between themselves mirrors and symbolizes the love that God shows for all His children.

Some professionals within our major social institutions claim that these social institutions' operational plans are blueprints for violence and insanity. Their policies trigger the violence experienced in the home and on the street. Similar to a colony of crazed ants that has lost its bedrock sense of survival, we are by degrees destroying ourselves in a fitful and mindless frenzy of anger, hostility, rage, destructiveness and violence. If we consider how much of our resources, particularly our monetary resources, Congress allocates for conveniences rather than for the improvement and quality of individual and family life, then it does appear that individual people have a low priority in our society.

Fostering intensive competition frequently

creates false goals. A competitive society which continuously extols individual goals is an immature society. Persons compete for money, power, prestige, and possessions, and such competition can frequently engender and nurture anger and violent feelings.

It is impossible to compete for a sense of personal worth, a desire to achieve for the good of the entire social order, a commitment to bring out the best in other people, a will to improve the quality of life instead of mere quantity, for these achievements are a matter of personal growth, realized and actualized within the individual. Competition often merely reflects external requirements but usually does not come to grips with the inner person. It can easily lead—and often does lead—to a dehumanized universe for it robs personality of over-all personal growth.

Technology, or the mechanization of the universe, will never enhance the course of peoples' lives through a greater qualitative fulfillment. The ever-advancing and ever-widening technology experienced daily reflects the search for external answers to external problems. Persons must re-educate themselves to reach within themselves for a re-affirmation of their own integrity and sovereignty over mechanical inventions.

Intuitively, people know they were created and ought to live for higher goals. A human who feels dominated by inhuman inventions can only experience anger and rage, which vent themselves in violent actions. Only by reaffirming his own place within the context of God's creative beauty will he experience his own presence, strength, harmony, love, accomplishment, and true human advancement.

Once an individual rediscovers his own unique beauty and direction in life by encountering who he is within the panoply of God's designs, only then can he use technology and mechanical inventions to achieve a goal that will benefit him and his family life. The other choice—the submission to blind mechanical inventions—can only lead to an escalating anger and, as a consequence, violent acts will eventually destroy what so many have worked so hard to build, namely, a just and peaceful social order. Violence in the home can be evaluated in relation to the wider problem of institutional operational plans, which in themselves may engender the very violence that they are trying to control.[23]

If these reflections are true about our social institutions, then the responsible personnel in these institutions need to re-examine carefully their priorities to ensure that the human person is Number One. Positive change in the programs of these institutions aimed at aiding persons may enhance immeasurably individual development and consequently create a more cooperative and humane social order.

The main thrust of this book has shown that violence is often learned in the family context.

The behavior observed, learned and practiced within the family unit has a pervasive and per-during influence on the family members. If we are going to have and enjoy a less violent society, violence among family members must be reduced or practically eliminated.

Persons who are socialized early in life to see and believe that violence contains positive pay-offs are formed to use force and violence in their interpersonal relationships to realize their goals. But if they develop other resourceful behavior, such as, affection, cooperation and communication, rather than force and violence, they are much more likely to build loving family relationships.

A viable avenue to reduce force and violence in the home as well as to enrich a family's life together are the various marriage enrichment programs. Most of these extend from one day to a weekend and explain various techniques of communication by which a husband and wife become more open and genuine, more understanding and accepting, more loving and intimate with one another. They are not problem-solving sessions, nor do they offer marriage counseling, but rather emphasize the husband and wife's ability to become more intimate and satisfied in their relationship through their own personal, mutual and reciprocal sharing.

Having personally been involved for several years with the National Marriage Encounter Movement, one experiences the closeness and intimacy which couples find as a result of their mutual empathy and decision to be lovers. The weekened is basically a crash course in communication. The presentations—made by three couples and a priest, minister or rabbi—are basically self revelations about their personal feelings and experiences. The participants progress from self examination, self definition and self discovery to a concentration on the husband and wife marital bond and on understanding and reaching out to God and others. It is a practical program built on a husband and wife's private dialoguing that enlivens their love for one another.

There is no gimmickry. The husband and wife are given the safe opportunity to really be themselves to one another. They divulge their fears, hopes, inadequacies and joys in the safety of a one-on-one private dialogue. The only group experience is when the three couples and the priest, minister or rabbi deliver their down-to-earth, non-preachy presentations.

The atmosphere of the weekend is one of mutuality and reciprocity. It is not a classroom, or a sensitivity session. Non-paid volunteer couples honestly and openly share who they are and how they live their married life. A husband may share how his overtime dedication to his career soured into feelings of inadequacy when he did not receive his hoped for promotion and raise. A wife may share how her easy going attitudes early in marriage turned into feelings of helplessness later on. The volunteer couples share how these feelings affected their marriage causing disillusionment and distance.

These are not confessions, but rather aid the listening couples to wrestle with and mutually share their own feelings and attitudes so that they may understand and accept one another. The encountering couples are urged by example to drop their masks of masculinity and femininity, fatherhood and motherhood, or the mask of the perfect marriage or the mask of no mask to be truly who they are. An admission by the men of the need for intimacy produces an atmosphere of trust and openness.

The Marriage Encounter weekend is not a panacea for every marital problem, but it does offer an exciting and informative insight into how to live happy, fulfilling marital lives. The weekend is not billed as a one-shot experience or is it terminated on a Sunday evening. The techniques that are learned and the spirit that is acquired on the weekend should motivate the encountered couples to join a support group in their neighborhood.

They can participate in community nights, image groups, rap sessions and a host of social gatherings. There are also various jobs within the voluntary, non-profit organization, such as, helping with the newsletter, recruiting new couples, hosting information parties, greeting couples as they prepare themselves to make a weekend as well as receiving the necessary training to be one of the three experienced couples who give presentations at future encounters.

Marriage enrichment programs, such as, National Marriage Encounter can help couples to become more intimate and sharing. These programs can lessen or release tensions and disillusionments within marriage so that men in particular will not resort to force or violence. It's difficult or almost impossible to be physically violent when the couple is holding hands or when the growing resentments are shared daily so as not to fester and eventually erupt into physical beatings.

Obviously anger or the inability to constructively deal with anger in a relationship often precipitates wife-beating episodes. When a husband and wife recognize their angry feelings rising, a healthy alternative to permitting their angry feelings from erupting into a violent brawl is to ask the partner for help in handling healthily these feelings. This asking for the partner's help brings the anger out into the open and aids the partner in applying the compassionate salve of healing love.

FOOTNOTES

1. Assaults, Felonious. File # 41. Complaint # 13626. Washtenaw County Sheriff's Department. July, 1974. Ann Arbor, Michigan.

2. Bard, M. Family Crisis Intervention: From Concept to Implementation. L.E.A.A. Grant NI 70-68.

3. Bart, P.B. Rape Doesn't End with a Kiss. Viva. June, 1975. 39-42 and 100-102.

4. Bell, J.N. New Hope for the Battered Wife. Good Housekeeping. August, 1976. 94-95 and 133-138.

5. Bickman, L. Bystander Intervention in a Crime. Paper presented at International Advanced Study Institute on Victimology and the Needs of Contemporary Society. Bellagio. Italy July, 1975.

6. Bonner, A. Wife Beating on the Rise. Washington Post. November 19, 1975.

7. Boston Globe. Home Strife Number One Cause of Murders in Atlanta. February 6, 1973.

8. Burgess, A.W. and Holmstrom, L.L. Rape: Victims of Crisis. Bowie, Maryland. Robert S. Brady Co. 1975.

9. Burton, Gabrielle. I'm Running Away From Home, But I'm Not Allowed to Cross the Street. New York: Avon Books. 1972.

10. Calvert, R. Criminal and Civil Liability in Husband-Wife Assaults in S. Steinmetz and M. Straus (eds.) Violence in the Family. New York: Harper and Row. 1974. 88-90.

11. Clasen, C. A Guide for Assaulted Women. Ann Arbor, Michigan: NOW Wife Assault Program. 1976.

12. Coote, A. Police, the Law, and Battered Wives. Manchester Guardian 2. May 23, 1974.

13. Curtis, L.A. Criminal Violence: National Patterns and Behavior. Lexington, Mass: Lexington Books. 1974.

14. Dalton, W. Wife Beating: Serious Issue. The Ypsilanti Press. April 9, 1975.

15. Davis, A.S. Sexual Assaults in the Philadelphia Prison System in John H. Gagnon and William Simon (eds.) The Sexual Scene. Chicago: Aldine. 1970.

16. Deutsch, H. The Significance of Masochism in the Mental Life of Woman. International Journal of Psycho-Analysis. XI. 1930.

17. Duncan, E. Half Way to Hope. The Citizen. Ottawa. August 12, 1976.

18. Edmiston, S. The Wife Beaters. Woman's Day. March, 1976.

19. Eideberg, L., M.D. Neurotic Choice of Mate in Victor W. Eisenstein, M.D. (ed.) Neurotic Interaction in Marriage. New York: Basic Books, Inc. 1956.

20. Eron, L.D., Leopold, O.W. and Lefkowitz. Learning of Aggression in Children. Boston: Little, Brown. 1971.

21. Federal Bureau of Investigation. Uniform Crime Reports for 1971. U.S. Government Printing Office. Washington, D.C. 1972.

22. Ferdon, J.J. Annual Report to the Mayor, San Francisco. July 1, 1973—June 30, 1974.

23. Fill, J.H. The Mental Breakdown of a Nation. New

York: New Viewpoints. A Division of Franklin Watts, Inc. 1974.

24. Field, M.H. and Field, H.F. Marital Violence and the Criminal Justice Process: Neither Justice nor Peace. The Social Service Review. 47. June, 1973. 221-240.

25. Fojtik, K.M. Wife Beating: How to Develop a Wife Assault Task Force and Project. Ann Arbor-Washtenaw County, Michigan 1976.

26. Fontana, V.J. The Maltreated Child: The Maltreatment Syndrome in Children. Springfield, Illinois. Charles C. Thomas. 1964.

27. Gayford, J.J. Wife Battering: A Preliminary Survey of 100 cases. British Medical Journal. 1. January 25, 1975. 194-197.

28. Gelles, R.J. An Exploratory Study of Intra-Family Violence. University of New Hampshire. Durham, N.H. Doctoral dissertation.

29. Gelles, R.J. Child Abuse as Psychopathology, A Sociological Critique and Reformulation. A paper presented at the annual meeting of the American Sociological Association. August, 1972.

30. Gelles, R.J. Child Abuse as Psychopathology: A Sociological Critique and Reformulation. American Journal of Orthopsychiatry. 43.4. July, 1973. 611-621.

31. Gelles, R.J. The Violent Home: A Study of Physical Aggression between Husbands and Wives. California: Sage Publications. 1974.

32. Gelles, R.J. Violence and Pregnancy: A Note on the Extent of the Problem and Need Services. The Family Coordinator. January, 1975. 81-86.

33. Gelles, R.J. The Social Construction of Child Abuse. American Journal of Orthopsychiatry. 45.3. April, 1975. 363-371.

34. Gelles, R.J. and Straus, M.A. Family Experience and Public Support of the Death Penalty. American Journal of Orthopsychiatry. 45.4. July, 1975. 596-613.

35. Gelles, R.J. On the Association of Sex and Violence in the Fantasy Production of College Students. Suicide. 5.2. Summer, 1975. 78-85.

36. Gill, D.G. Violence Against Children in S. Steinmetz and M. Straus (eds.) Violence in the Family. New York: Harper and Row. 1974. 141-147.

37. Gottlieb, M. Crime Report on New York City. New York: Daily News. August 21, 1976.

38. Gunn, J. Violence New York: Praeger Publishers. 1973.

39. Hartzler versus City of San Jose. 46 C.A. 3rd 6. California Reporter. 1975.

40. Horney, K., M.D. Feminine Psychology. Harold Kelman, M.D. (ed.) New York: W.W. Norton and Company, Inc. 1973.

41. Huggins, M.D. and Straus, M.A. Violence and the Social Structure as Reflected in Children's Books from 1850 to 1970. November 26, 1974.

42. Jackson, S. In Search of Equal Protection for Battered Wives. Unpublished Monograph. 1975.

43. Kahan, S. Beaten Wives Masochistic? I Don't Believe It. The Observer Eccentric. June 12, 1975.

44. Kalamazoo Study: Wife Beating Women Against Violence Against Women. 1976.

45. Kansas City Police Department. Conflict Management: Analysis/Resolution. 1973.

46. Katz, S. Battered Wives Seeking Refuge. The Toronto Star. August 23, 1975.

47. Kolb, T.M. and Straus, M.A. Marital Power and Marital Happiness in Relation to Problem-Solving Ability. Journal of Marriage and the Family. November, 1974. 756-766.

48. Krolik, C. No Legal Protection From Husband Assault. Michigan Free Press. April 14, 1975.

49. Kuhn, M.A. There's No Place Like Home for Beatings and Murders. Washington Evening Star. November 11, 1975.

50. Laing, R.D. The Politics of the Family. New York: Vintage Books. 1972.

51. Levinger, G. Sources of Marital Dissatisfaction Among Applicants for Divorce 126-132. Families in Crisis. New York: Harper and Row. 1970.

52. Light, R. Abused and Neglected Children in America: A Study of Alternative Policies. Harvard Educational Review. 43. November. 556-598.

53. Mahler, M.S., M.D. and Rabinovitch, R., M.D. The Effects of Marital Conflict on Child Development in Victor W. Eisenstein (ed.) Neurotic Interaction in Marriage. New York: Basic Books, Inc. 1956.

54. May, R. Power and Innocence. New York: W.W. Norton and Co. 1972.

55. Michelow, P. and Eisenberg, S. The Assaulted Wife: Catch 22 Revisited. (A Preliminary Overview of Wife-Beating in Michigan) copyright 1974. Unpublished. University of Michigan Law School.

56. Michener, J.A. The Kent State Four/Should Have Studied More in S. Steinmetz and M. Straus (eds.) Violence in the Family. New York: Harper and Row, 1974, 180-187.

57. Mill, J.S. The Subjection of Women. London: Oxford University Press. 1912.

58. Mondale Bill on Child Abuse Prevention and Treatment Act of 1973 (PL 93-247).

59. Morris, J. Her Husband Finally in Jail. Detroit Free Press, November 3, 1975.

60. Mydans, S. Wife Beating: Ann Arbor News. July 28, 1975.

61. Myers, J. The Beaten Wife. Ann Arbor News. September 18, 1975.

62. Nolan, T. Wife Beating Surfaces in Suburbia. Fairpress. August 11, 1976.

63. Northrup, B. Battered Women: Wife-Beating Persists but British Attack It. The Wall Street Journal. August 20, 1976.

64. O'Brien, J. Violence in Divorce Prone Families. Journal of Marriage and the Family 33. 1971. 692-698.

65. Palmer, S. Physical Frustration and Murder in S. Steinmetz and M. Straus (eds.) Violence in the Family. New York. Harper and Row. 1974. 247-250.

66. Parnas, R.I. The Police Response to the Domestic Disturbance. Wisconsin Law Review. 914. Fall 1967. 914-960.

67. Parnas, R. Police Discretion and Diversion of Incidents of Intrafamily Violence. Law and Contemporary Problems. 36. 1971.

68. Parnas, R. The Violent Society. New Haven: College and University Press. 1972.

69. Peterson, W. System Frustrates Battered Wives. Washington Post. November 2, 1975.

70. Pizzy, E. Scream Quietly or the Neighbors Will Hear. London. Penguin Press. 1974.

71. Pogrebin, L.C. Do Women Make Men Violent? MS: 3 November 1974. 49-55 and 80.

72. Radbill, S.X. A History of Child Abuse and Infanticide in S. Steinmetz and M. Straus (eds.) Violence in the Family. New York. Harper and Row. 1974. 173-179.

73. Rado, S. Fear of Castration in Women. Psycho-Analytic Quarterly III-IV. 1933.

74. Rainbow Retreat, Inc. What's It All About? Phoenix, Arizona. November, 1975.

75. Resnick, P. Child Murder by Parents: A Psychiatric Review of Filicide. American Journal of Psychiatry. 126.3. 1969. 325-334.

76. Resnick, J. Wife Beating. Counselor Training Manual # 1. Women Against Violence Against Women. 1976.

77. Rosenthall, A.M. Thirty-Eight Witnesses. N.Y.: McGraw Hill. 1964.

78. Russell, C. Violence in the Family Is As Typical As Love. Washington Evening Star. February 24, 1976.

79. Ryder, R.G. Husband-Wife Dyads versus Married Strangers. Family Process. 1968. 233-237.

80. Sacramento Bee. Police Intervention. July 8, 1972.

81. Schultz, L.G. The Wife Assaulter. Journal of Social Psychiatry. 6.2. 1960. 103-112.

82. Sears, R.R., Macoby, E.E. and Levin, H. Patterns of Child Rearing. Evanston: Row, Peterson. 1957.

83. Shearer, L. Ingeborg Dedichen: She Was the Great Love of Aristotle Onassis. Parade. July 20, 1975. 4-5.

84. Snell, J.E., M.D., Rosenwald, R.J., M.D. and Robey, A., M.D. The Wifebeater's Wife: A Study of Family Interaction. Archives of General Psychiatry. 11 August, 1964. 107-112.

85. Steele, B. and Pollack, C. A Psychiatric Study of Parents who Abuse Infants and Small Children. in R. Helfer and C. Kempe (eds.) The Battered Child. Chicago: University of Chicago Press. 1968.

86. Steinmetz, S.K. Occupation and Physical Punishment: A Response to Stress. Journal of Marriage and the Family. 33. November 1971. 664-665.

87. Steinmetz, S.K. and Straus, M.A. (editors) Violence in the Family. New York: Harper and Row. 1974.

88. Steinmetz, S.K. and Straus, M.A. Intrafamilial Patterns of Conflict Resolution: U.S. and Canadian Comparisons. A paper presented at the Annual Meeting of the Society for the Study of Social Problems. 1975.

89. Straus, M.A. Some Social Antecedents of Physical Punishment: A Linkage Theory Interpretation. Journal of Marriage and the Family. November, 1971. 658-663.

90. Straus, M.A. Cultural and Social Organizational Influences on Violence Between Family Members. R. Prime and D. Barried (eds.). in Configurations: Biological and Cultural Factors in Sexuality and Family Life. New York: D.C. Heath. Lexington Books. 1972. 53-69.

91. Straus, M.A. A General System Theory Approach to a Theory of Violence between Family Members. Social Science Information. 12.3. June, 1973. 105-125.

92. Straus, M.A Leveling Civility and Violence in the Family. Journal of Marriage and the Family. 36. February, 1974. 13-29.

93. Straus, M.A. Societal Morphogenesis and Intrafamily Violence in Cross-Cultural Perspective. Annals of the New York Academy of Sciences. 1976.

94. Straus, M.A. Sexual Inadequacy, Cultural Norms and Wife Beating. Victimology. 1.1. 1976.

95. Straus, M.A. Societal Morphogenesis and Intrafamily Violence in Cross-Cultural Perspective. Annals of the New York Academy of Sciences. 1976 (in press).

96. Survey of Public Attitudes Toward Police Services. City Planning Commission. New Haven, Connecticut. February, 1970.

97. Tardiff, K.J., M.D., M.P.H. A Survey of Psychiatrists in Boston and Their Work with Violent Patients. American Journal of Psychiatry. 131.9. September, 1974. 1008-1011.

98. The Guardian. The Children of Violence. April 22, 1976.

99. Truninger, E. Marital Violence: The Legal Solutions. Hastings Law Journal. 23. November, 1976. 259-276.

100. U.S. News and World Report. Battered Wives: Now They're Fighting Back. September 20, 1976. 47-49.

101. Weinraub, J. The Battered Wives of England: Place to Heal Their Wounds. The New York Times. November 29, 1975.

102. Williams, R.M. American Society: A Sociological Interpretation. N.Y.: Alfred A. Knopf. 1970.

103. Winter, W.D., Ferreira, A.J. and Bowers, N. Decision-Making in Married and Unrelated Couples. Family Process. 1973. 12: 83-94.

104. Wolfgang, M.E. Husband-Wife Homicides. Corrective Psychiatry and Journal of Social Theraphy. 2. 1956. 263-271.

105. Zintl, T. Ann Arbor Now Shelters Battered Wives. Detroit Free Press. August 29, 1975.

106. Zintl, T. Wife Abuse: Our Almost-Hidden Social Problem. Detroit Free Press. January 25, 1976.

107. Zullo, A.A. and Fulman, R. Wife-Beating In "Nice" Homes. New Woman. March-April, 1976. 68-69.

USEFUL ADDRESSES

Here are names and addresses, in your area or near it, which you can write or call for assistance such as counseling, advocacy programs, emergency rescue service, or (occasionally) residence for you and your children. Answers to your enquiries will specify what help is being offered in each case. We wish to thank the Editors of MS MAGAZINE for their courtesy in allowing us to use this list.

NATIONAL:

Center for Women Policy Studies
2000 P St. N.W. Suite 508
Washington, D.C. 20007
202-872-1770

National Organization for Women
National Task Force on Battered Women
651 Duncan St.
San Francisco, CA. 94131
415-928-2480

7 Aloha Drive
Pittsburgh, PA. 15239
412-327-5077

REGIONAL:

Arizona:
Rainbow Retreat Inc.
513 W. Latham
Phoenix, Arizona 85003

California:
Haven House Inc.
644 S. Marengo Ave. Pasadena, CA. 91106
213-681-2626

La Casa de las Madres
1800 Market St. Box 137, San Francisco, CA. 94102
415-626-7859

Women's Transitional Living Center
c/o Susan Maples, Director, Community Development
Council
1140 S. Bristol St., Santa Anna, CA. 92704
714-992-1931

Florida:
Fort Lauderdale Police Dept. Victim Advocate Office
1300 W. Broward Blvd. Fort Lauderdale, Fla. 33312
305-761-2143

Citizens Dispute Settlement Center
Metro Justice Bldg. 1351 N.W. 12th. St. Miami, Fla.
33125
305-547-7062

Task Force on Battered Women
YWCA 100 S.E. 4th. St. Miami, Fla. 33168
305-377-8161

Women in Distress, Jackson Memorial Hospital
122 N.E. 24th. St. Miami, Fla. 33137
305-573-5528

Maryland:
Battered Wives Task Force
5403 Queens Chapel Rd. West Hyattsville, MD. 20782
202-WA7-5877

Massachusetts:
Women's Transition House
46 Pleasant St. Cambridge, Mass. 02139
617-547-5942

Elizabeth Stone House
128 Minden St. Jamaica Plains, Mass. 02130
617-522-3417

Respond Inc.
Box 555, Somerville Mass. 02134
617-776-5931

Michigan:
NOW Domestic Violence/Spouse Assault Task Force
1917 Washtenaw Ave. Ann Arbor, Mich. 48104
313-995-5444

Minnesota:
Women's Advocates
584 Grand Ave. St. Paul, Minn. 55102
612-227-8284

New York:
South Brooklyn Legal Services
152 Court St. Brooklyn, N.Y. 11201
212-855-8003

Abused Women's Aid in Crisis
Maria Roy, Foundress
P.O. Box 431, Cathedral Station, New York, N.Y.
10025
212-473-8181 or 212-473-8182 (hot line)

Family Counseling Center
238-10 Hillside Avenue
Bellerose, N.Y. 11426
IN-3-3679

Oregon:
Bradley Angel House
c/o Women's Place, 1915 N.E. Everett, Portland, Ore.
97232
503-243-7044

Pennsylvania:
Women's Center South
2929 Brownsville Rd.
Brentwood, PA. 14227
412-885-2888

Women Against Abuse
Women's Center, 5519 Wister St. Philadelphia, PA.
19144
215-848-7327

Washington:
Women's Emergency Housing Project
1012 W. 12th. St. Vancouver, Wash. 98660
206-695-0501 or 206-694-8366

Wisconsin:
Women's Coalition Inc.
2211 E. Kenwood Blvd. Milwaukee, Wis. 53211
414-964-6177 or 414-964-7535 (after 5 p.m.)

Canada:
Interval House
596 Huron St. Toronto, Canada. M5R 2R7
416-924-1491